COVERT ACTION

MICHAEL KRONENWETTER

COVERT ACTION

An Impact Book
Franklin Watts   1991
New York   London   Toronto   Sydney

Photographs courtesy of: Historical Pictures Service, Chicago: p. 23; AP/
Wide World Photos: pp. 36, 42, 61, 70, 78, 85, 88, 91, 93; UPI/Bettmann
Newsphotos: pp. 67, 76, 121.

Library of Congress Cataloging-in-Publication Data

Kronenwetter, Michael.
    Covert action / Michael Kronenwetter.
       p. cm.—(An Impact book)
    Includes bibliographical references and index.
    Summary: Presents the history of the real "cloak-and-dagger" world
of espionage as OSS and CIA agents carry out covert intelligence
operations to further American foreign and military policy.
    ISBN 0-531-13018-5
    1. Intelligence service—United States—History—Juvenile
literature. 2. Espionage, American—History—Juvenile literature.
3. United States. Office of Strategic Services—History—Juvenile
literature. 4. United States. Central Intelligence Agency—
History—Juvenile literature. [1. Intelligence service—History.
2. Espionage, American—History. 3. United States. Office of
Strategic Services.—History. 4. United States. Central
Intelligence Agency.—History.] I. Title.
HV6431.K69 1991
327.12'0973—dc20   90-46209 CIP AC

CONTENTS

1

CLOAK AND DAGGER

The world is in peril! Only the quick action of one highly skilled and dedicated secret agent can save it.

Major Sam, the power-mad leader of Ste. Margaritte, a small island in the western Caribbean, has gotten his hands on a new, immensely radio-active kind of nuclear weapon. It is hidden somewhere in the world, set to explode at a signal from Ste. Margaritte.

If that weapon ever goes off, it will spread deadly radiation around the globe. Only the people of Ste. Margaritte—protected by a radiation-proof shield Major Sam has built over their little island—will survive.

American intelligence has learned that Major Sam plans to detonate the weapon in two days. Except for Ste. Margaritte, the world will be destroyed. What is there to do? There is no hope of sending American forces to capture the insane major, or even to destroy Ste. Margaritte. Any approaching U.S. ship or plane would be spotted by the island's sophisticated radar system. And Major Sam is bound to explode his bomb at the first sign of danger.

The American president decides that there is only

one hope for the world—the slim possibility that a single daring individual can somehow sneak into Ste. Margaritte, disarm the deadly weapon, and "neutralize" the demented major.

There is only one person for the job—America's most experienced and dedicated secret agent, Jake Hero. Jake is America's James Bond. He has the body and skills of a highly trained athlete, the brain of a rocket scientist, the quick wits of a chess master, and the nerves of a cat burglar.

Jake is parachuted into the waters off Ste. Margaritte, wearing scuba gear. Finding the great shield over the island already in place, he circles the island underwater until he comes to a cave. Exploring it, he finds that it leads to a small lake far inland.

He surfaces to find the lake deserted, except for a beautiful woman sunbathing on the beach. She is shocked to see him, but he uses his enormous charm to befriend her. She is, he is pleased to find out, one of the many residents of Ste. Margaritte who hate Major Sam.

The lovely sunbather directs Jake to the dictator's fabulous mansion high on a mountain on the far side of the island. The entrance to the mansion is guarded by members of the island's security force. They are heavily armed, but Jake quickly overwhelms them, using his advanced training in martial arts.

Inside the mansion, Jake finds his way to the basement control center. He disables the security men in silent hand-to-hand combat and quickly finds the long-distance firing mechanism, primed to be used to set off the hidden bomb. Using his tremendous store of technical knowledge, Jake rapidly disarms the switch, making the weapon impossible to detonate.

The world is safe—at least for now. But Jake's mission is not yet done. The heroic agent makes his way to Major Sam's luxurious bedroom, where he finds the insane ruler deep asleep. Waking him, Jake forces the major to lead him to the mansion's underground parking garage. From the many high-powered automobiles they find there, Jake selects the fastest—a tailor-made 12-cylinder Maserati.

Jake orders the major to drive to the coast, where he plans to rendezvous with the submarine lurking offshore to pick him up. But security patrols spot the racing car and give chase. Jake orders the major to drive faster and faster over the sharply curving road that leads down the mountain.

But Major Sam has no intention of remaining a prisoner. As the speeding car approaches the sharpest curve on the road, he straightens the wheels. Laughing wildly, he drives the car off the road and over a cliff, 300 yards above a rocky beach.

With the car quickly losing its forward momentum and sliding into a sickening drop, Jake shrugs. Opening the door, he waves good-bye to the doomed dictator and leaps out. As the car smashes to pieces on the rocks below, Jake activates a portable solar-powered rocket backpack and soars out over the ocean.

Flying around the island, he gently lowers himself to the water over the waiting sub. Removing his backpack and taking a deep breath, he swims down to the sub and is soon heading happily for home.

He has saved earth from destruction. And no one but the president and a few trusted advisers will ever know.

That is the cloak-and-dagger world of the secret agent—the world of covert action—as it is portrayed in movies, in adventure novels, in comic books, and on television. It is a world of danger, excitement, and violence. Most of all, it is a world of fantasy.

But there is a real world of covert action as well. It is a world in which the foreign policy of the United States and other countries is carried out in secret, in ways ordinary citizens are never told about, by people they never know exist. What is done in that secret world helps shape the greater world we all live in. But it shapes it in ways that few citizens understand, for reasons that are rarely, if ever, explained.

In this book, we will look at the way the real cloak-and-dagger world operates. We will find out how much it resembles the fantasy world we know from the movies. We will look at covert action's place in American history. We will examine some of its greatest successes and its most disastrous failures. And we will ask some fundamental questions about it.

DEFINING COVERT ACTION

Covert means "hidden," "protected," or, better yet, "covered up." Within the U.S. government, the term "covert action" is used more or less interchangeably with "covert operations," "covert activities," and even "special activities." All are used to refer to actions of the government, carried out in secret, designed to promote the goals and interests of the United States.

One of the first official descriptions of covert action was contained in a directive signed by President Harry Truman in 1948. It referred to a wide variety of "covert activities." They ranged from such relatively peaceful pursuits as propaganda to "sabotage, anti-sabotage, demolition and evacuation measures"; and from "economic warfare" to "subversion against hostile states" or "support of indigenous anti-communist elements in threatened countries of the free world." They also included "preventative direct action," as well as assistance to underground resistance movements, guerrillas and refugee liberation groups."[1]

Some three decades later, a Senate committee gave a very broad explanation of covert action, defining it as "any clandestine [secret] activity designed to influence foreign governments, events, organizations, or persons in support of United States foreign policy. Covert action may include political and economic actions, propaganda, and paramilitary activities."[2] (The term *paramilitary* refers to any armed force that is not a part of a country's acknowledged military organizations.)

INTELLIGENCE

There has always been a close relationship between covert activities and the gathering of intelligence.

For most of us, the word *intelligence* means the human ability to think. For those in government, however, intelligence means information—the bits and pieces of fact that make up a picture of the world and what is happening in it. The government agencies responsible for collecting these facts, and for putting them together and deciding what they mean, are called intelligence agencies.

When the intelligence collected is information another government wants to keep secret, intelligence gathering is known as spying, or espionage. Spying is an ancient practice. There have probably been professional spies as long as there have been governments. Over 2,000 years ago, Chinese emperors already had elaborate systems of spies operating throughout their territories and beyond.

There are obvious connections between intelligence and covert action. Those who spy and those who carry out covert activities use many of the same techniques and tactics. Both act in secrecy. Both traditionally work in foreign countries, where they do things their hosts would consider highly illegal.

But intelligence gathering and covert action are two different things. Their methods are sometimes similar, but their purposes are different. The object of gathering intelligence is essentially passive. It involves finding out about the world as it is. Covert action, on the other hand, involves changing things. Spying provides information to help the government *decide* what it should do. Covert action helps the government do it.

The line between the two is sometimes narrow, but it is there. Bribing foreign officials to learn their government's plans is spying. Bribing the same officials to *influence* their government's plans is covert action.

Historically, as we will see, covert action grew up within intelligence agencies. Even today, it is considered a part of the overall intelligence community. In fact, the government agency responsible for America's covert action operations is also responsible for many foreign espionage activities. It is known as the Central Intelligence Agency, or CIA. The CIA is far from the largest or best-funded of the government's intelligence agencies. But it is far and away the biggest practitioner of covert action.

THE PURPOSES OF COVERT ACTION

Covert activities can take place either inside or outside the country. Traditionally, however, they are usually carried out abroad. That is partly because covert action is used primarily as a tool of foreign policy, and partly because the CIA is forbidden by law to act inside the United States.

In practice, covert actions are usually designed to accomplish one or more of the following things:

Give help to friendly governments. Covert help to foreign governments often includes undercover shipments of money or weapons. It may also involve the training of foreign military forces, police, or antiterrorist forces, especially those engaged in fighting Communists and others considered enemies of the United States.

Give help to friendly politicians. The United States often helps particular foreign leaders, or potential leaders, that it hopes will be helpful to U.S. interests. This secret help can include anything from political advice to economic or technical assistance. Sophisticated propaganda efforts have been launched to promote the careers of friendly foreign politicians, and secret contributions have been made to their election campaigns.

Hurt America's enemies. Many of the same tactics used to help America's friends are also used to hurt America's enemies. Since World War II, "enemies" has usually meant Communist governments and Communist movements around the world. In addition to the political and propaganda tactics mentioned above, more extreme measures are sometimes used. These include efforts to undermine the economies of hostile countries or to reduce the value of their currencies. In many cases, rebels fighting foreign governments have been advised, trained, and supplied by the United States. In extreme cases, the United States has even launched paramilitary operations of its own against such governments.

Promote America's economic or political interests. This is a broad, catchall category that includes everything from paramilitary raids against terrorists to propaganda operations designed to promote pro–U.S. feeling abroad. It may also include paying bribes to foreign officials or members of the media, placing American agents in positions of power abroad, or recruiting foreign leaders to act as American agents.

"PLAUSIBLE DENIABILITY"

All covert actions are carried out in secret, but it is a special kind of secrecy. It is not primarily designed to conceal what is being done. (How could you conceal the fact that a paramilitary force is invading a country, for example?) Instead, it is designed to conceal the *responsibility* for what is being done.

President Truman's 1948 directive made this purpose clear. It ordered that covert actions be "so planned and executed that any US [sic] Government responsibility for them is not evident to unauthorized persons and that if uncovered the US Government can plausibly disclaim any responsibility for them."[3]

The Senate committee later made the purpose even clearer. It explained that covert actions were "planned and executed . . . to conceal the identity of the sponsor" and "to permit the sponsor's plausible denial of the operation."[4] A "plausible" denial is one that is reasonably believable, no matter how untrue it may be.

The terms "plausible denial" and "plausible deniability" are basic to the concept of covert action. They mean that even if a government covert action is exposed, the government can claim that it had nothing to do with it. It can "plausibly deny" any responsibility for what it has done. At least in theory, it can escape the natural consequences of its actions. And that is what covert action is all about.

14

2

THE BEGINNINGS OF COVERT ACTION

Any account of the role of covert action in American history is bound to be incomplete. By definition, covert activities are carried out in secret. In some cases, even the targets of successful covert actions never find out exactly what happened to them, or who was responsible for it.

This secrecy makes it hard to find out about covert activities. As a rule, the people who take part in them are sworn not to reveal what they know. When people join the Central Intelligence Agency, for instance, they sign an oath promising they will let the CIA review, and censor, in advance anything they ever plan to publish about their time with the Agency.

Still, many covert actions do eventually come to light. This happens in various ways. The government gives out information about some covert operations itself. President Jimmy Carter, for example, publicly admitted the failure of a secret military mission to rescue American hostages being held in Iran in April 1980.

More often, however, covert actions are revealed by others—often by those who were their targets. When Cuban exiles launched an invasion of Cuba in 1961, the governments of Cuba and the Soviet Union charged that the CIA had been behind it.

Although the U.S. State Department officially denied the United States had been involved, President John Kennedy publicly took responsibility for the invasion's failure.[1]

Journalists uncover some covert activities as part of their effort to keep the public informed of what the government is doing. Bob Woodward's book *Veil*, for example, did a lot to explain the inner workings at the top level of the CIA during the 1980s.[2]

Members of Congress, and congressional committees, occasionally make some aspects of covert activities public while carrying out their role as overseers of all government agencies. This usually happens when there is a conflict between the Congress and the executive branch agencies that carry out covert operations, such as the CIA. (This ongoing conflict will be discussed in detail later in this book.)

Some of the most revealing accounts of covert activities come from the people who helped to carry them out. Scores, if not hundreds, of books and articles have been written by veterans of covert action. Many of them have been used as sources for this book. Some of their names can be found in the For Further Reading section.

No matter how the story of a covert action comes to light, there is no way to be sure that the story is both accurate and complete. Certainly the targets of covert operations have to be considered less than reliable as witnesses. Most of them are politically hostile to the United States to begin with. The possibility that they have been made the victims of U.S. covert operations can only make them more hostile than ever. It would be foolish to assume that they would not lie, or at least exaggerate, to make the United States look bad.

At best, the press discovers only a few aspects of

any covert actions. The real purpose and extent of the operation often remain hidden. The journalists' information usually comes from "leaks" made by government officials. (A leak happens when someone releases information that is supposed to remain secret.) The officials who leak information about covert activities usually have secret motives of their own. Their leaks are partial at best, and the information is usually impossible to prove.

The ex-agents who publish accounts of their covert activities have their own axes to grind as well. Some, disillusioned veterans of covert action like Philip Agee and Victor Marchetti, are trying to make a case against their old profession. Others, who are proud of what they have done, like ex–CIA director William Colby, try to make a case in favor of it. Both might be suspected of slanting what they choose to tell in order to support their prejudices. After all, as covert agents, they are experienced in using propaganda.

Congressional committees may reveal some details of particular activities, but in general they respect the covert agencies' desire for secrecy. They rarely allow the full story of any covert operation to come out. They reveal only what they have to reveal in order to serve their own purposes, such as keeping an agency under some congressional control.

All of this does not mean that these sources never tell the truth. In many cases, they do. The problem for journalists, historians, and the public is that it is hard to be sure. There is usually no way to check the truth of these accounts. The proof, if any exists, is usually in the hands of the CIA, and the CIA almost never releases records that would prove or disprove anything about a covert activity. In fact, the CIA rarely comments on covert activities at all. When it does, its word is probably no more reliable than that of any of the other sources mentioned here.

Ironically, the CIA's devotion to secrecy makes it likely that more failures of covert action will be made public than successes. They are the operations that enemies of the covert action—the people most likely to reveal information about them—want exposed. The successes remain hidden in the files of the CIA or other covert action agencies, who refuse to release them.

It is probably true, then, that most covert actions, the successes and the failures alike, remain secret. And even what we know about those that have become public is limited. There are just too many people keeping too many secrets for us to ever be sure we have a complete picture of the world of covert action.

In this book, we will deal primarily with the best-publicized examples of covert operations. With a few exceptions, these are among the relatively few cases that have been widely discussed and debated by both supporters and opponents of covert action. They are the cases about which the most is known. Still, it must be remembered that any account of covert action is like a picture of a sea filled with icebergs: only the tips are visible. The viewer, or the reader, is left to guess how much ice is lurking beneath the surface.

THE EARLIEST COVERT ACTIVITIES

Even more than other agencies, the CIA is obsessed with secrecy. Officially, it rarely, if ever, comments on U.S. government covert activities. Ordinarily, it has little to say publicly about anything at all.

In 1976, however, the CIA was as caught up in the bicentennial spirit as the rest of the nation. The

U.S. was 200 years old, and the whole country was celebrating. Throughout the government, agencies were marking the occasion with books and other publications detailing their history. The CIA joined in with a few publications of its own, including one called *Intelligence in the War of Independence.*[3] In it, the Agency traces the history of American covert actions back to acts of sabotage at the time of the American Revolution. Clearly, the roots of covert action go very deep into the history of the United States.

The first president to resort to secrecy in carrying out American foreign policy was, in fact, George Washington. In 1790, the very first Congress voted money for a special fund the president could use to pay for secret missions. Congress made it clear that he would not be asked to explain publicly what he did with the money.[4]

Then, as now, secrecy in the conduct of foreign policy was controversial. Refusing to show Congress some documents it had asked for that were related to secret treaty negotiations, Washington explained that secrecy was necessary in diplomatic negotiations. Even after the negotiations were over, he insisted, "a full disclosure of all the measures . . . which may have been proposed or contemplated would be extremely impolitic [unwise]." According to intelligence expert William R. Corson, Washington's phrase "all the measures" was widely assumed "to mean the payments of bribes, etc., to insure the support of foreign leaders."[5]

MATHEWS'S ARMY

The first major example of a U.S. paramilitary covert action came in 1811. In that year, President James Madison was worried that war was about to break out with England. He was afraid that if it did, Spain would let England use her colony Florida as a base to attack the American South. Hoping to prevent that possibility, Madison sent George Mathews on a secret mission to Florida to take control of the Spanish colony for the United States.

An ex–Indian fighter, ex–American Revolutionary War officer and prisoner of war, ex-governor of the state of Georgia, and ex-member of Congress, Mathews was already an old man in 1811. But, like many other secret warriors who would come after him, he had a high opinion of himself—and of his value to his country. It was said he believed that no one except George Washington had done more for America than he had. Now, at the age of seventy-two, he was ready to do even more.

Mathews actually had two missions in Florida. The first was open and aboveboard. He was to try to negotiate a deal with Spain for Florida. It was only if Spain refused to deal that his second, covert, mission became active. That was to seize Florida from Spain. But he was to do it, if possible, without starting a war with Spain.

It didn't take long for Mathews to discover that Spain would not give up Florida. He returned to his home base in Georgia and recruited a ragtag group of veterans and adventurers into an unofficial army. By March 1812, he had persuaded some of the many English-speaking people who lived in Florida to proclaim its independence from Spain.

Mathews and his men now had an excuse for action. They were soon joined by some actual American troops, who claimed they had come as volunteers to help the Floridians.

Mathews's little army was not very large or powerful, but it was big enough to cause trouble for the poorly supplied Spanish forces in Florida. It might have actually succeeded in taking over the colony, except for the storm of controversy that news of its activities caused back home.

Madison had kept the operation so secret he hadn't even told James Monroe, his own secretary of state, about it. When word of the invasion of Florida got back to Washington, D.C., Monroe was outraged at the news. He sent word to end the fighting at once.

Publicly, Monroe announced that Mathews had *not* been acting on behalf of the U.S. government. He must have misunderstood his orders. This was the first example of "plausible deniability" at work. Mathews had actually been acting on the direct orders of the president of the United States.[6]

Mathews's Florida adventure marked many other firsts as well. It was the first time that U.S. agents stirred up foreign citizens to revolt against their government, and the first time that U.S. paramilitaries ever attempted to overthrow a foreign government by force. It was also the first time that an exposed covert action caused political embarrassment in Washington. As we will see in later chapters, it was far from the last.

GROWTH OF THE INTELLIGENCE COMMUNITY

The Constitution of the United States divided the federal government into three branches: the executive, the legislative, and the judicial. It described the powers each branch would have and reserved all other powers to the states or to the people. In all of this, it said nothing at all about covert operations.

Nonetheless, as we have seen, covert activities began almost immediately. And, from the beginning, the control of covert operations was in the

21

hands of the executive branch of government—that is, of the president.

It was Congress that voted for the special fund for covert activities in 1790, but it was President Washington who decided how the money should be spent. Later Congresses continued to provide funds for presidents to use for conducting the secret business of the United States. Sometimes presidents controlled these funds directly; sometimes they worked through their secretaries of state. From 1806 on, the money set aside for covert use was known in the federal budget as the Secret Service funds.[7]

One of the main uses nineteenth-century presidents made of these funds was sending personal representatives abroad. These representatives had a variety of duties. Some were diplomats sent abroad, without notifying Congress, to conduct tricky negotiations for the president. Others may have recruited spies and bribed foreign officials. Probably only a handful of them were involved in what we would call covert action.

The first formal secret government agency was founded in 1862, during the Civil War. Called the National Detective Police, its main job was to combat the Confederate spies that seemed to be everywhere in the Union, particularly in the capital, Washington. The agency was put under the command of a daring ex–Union spy named Lafayette C. Baker. When the secretary of war, Edwin Stanton, gave him the post, he told Baker that his job would be the "dirtiest of this dirty war."[8] He ordered Baker never to reveal the authority for his actions to anyone.

Stanton's desire for secrecy was understandable. The National Detective Police carried out several activities that were considered illegal. They included night raids on taverns, gambling dens, and

22

Lafayette C. Baker was head of the National Detective Police, the first formal secret government agency. Founded in 1862 during the Civil War, its mission was to combat Confederate spies.

houses of prostitution, along with sweeping arrests of thousands of suspected Confederate spies and sympathizers. Many of those captured were kept in prison for long periods without trial, sometimes on no evidence at all.

The National Detective Police was a secret organization, but it was not designed primarily for covert actions. Nonetheless, it paved the way for the covert action agencies to come. It showed that it was possible for a government agency to work in secrecy, and even outside the law. What is more, Baker established the basic argument that has been used to defend covert activities ever since. When the safety of the nation is at stake, he argued, any means are justified to preserve it—no matter how illegal or even immoral those means might otherwise be.

In 1865, the National Detective Police was transformed into a new agency called the Secret Service. Placed under the secretary of the treasury, its main job was to protect the nation's currency against counterfeiters. Following the assassination of President William McKinley in 1901, it was given the job of protecting the president and other high government officials as well.

Like the National Detective Police, the Secret Service was primarily a *counter*intelligence agency. That is, its main job was to protect against foreign spies and covert activities, rather than to carry out espionage and covert activities of its own.

In 1908, a new kind of intelligence agency took its place alongside the Secret Service. This one was in the Justice Department, and was known as the Bureau of Investigation. It would later become famous as the Federal Bureau of Investigation, or FBI.

The Bureau's main job was to carry out Justice Department investigations inside the United States. During its first decade, this meant mostly matters that had to do with interstate commerce laws, labor unions, and American political radicals. The original Bureau of Investigation was made up of agents brought over from the Secret Service. In time, however, the two agencies would develop their own loyalties.

Both the Bureau and the Secret Service were primarily domestic agencies; that is, most of the time they operated within the United States. The Secret Service, however, also sometimes acted abroad. In fact, it may have been the first non-military government agency to carry out illegal operations in a foreign country. In 1899, some of its agents in Montreal, Canada, committed several illegal acts in the process of exposing a Spanish spy ring there. They broke into the private apartment of a foreign diplomat and stole papers from it, and they may have forged evidence used against the Spanish spies as well.[9]

The military had always conducted espionage during wartime. From the Revolutionary War to the Civil War, they recruited spies and slipped agents behind enemy lines to scout out the territory and check on troop movements. Starting with the Civil War, the Army also had its own Signal Intelligence Corps, whose job was to intercept and interpret enemy messages. But it wasn't until 1882 that the first peacetime military intelligence department was established. That was when the Navy set up the Office of Naval Intelligence, or ONI. The new agency remained small and relatively ineffective until the Spanish-American War, of 1898.[10]

Once the Navy had an intelligence agency, the other military organizations wanted agencies of their own. The War Department established the Bureau of Military Intelligence in 1885, and the Army set up a separate intelligence division in 1889.[11]

25

That was the same year that Congress first voted funds to send military attachés abroad. These military officers were stationed at (or *attached* to) American embassies in foreign capitals. They served as U.S. military observers in the host countries. From the very beginning, their job served as an ideal "cover" for espionage—and eventually covert action—missions.[12]

The military intelligence agencies were not very large. Working separately and with little cooperation with each other, they were not very efficient either. In 1903, the G-2 division of the Military General Staff took central authority over all military intelligence. But G-2 turned out to be ineffective, and the arrangement eventually fell apart.[13] Eventually, when World War I broke out in Europe, overall control of foreign intelligence was put into the hands of the State Department.[14]

The war saw the U.S. intelligence community grow by leaps and bounds. Partly this was due to the war itself. (War always emphasizes the need for good intelligence.) But partly it was due to the Bolshevik Revolution, which took place in Russia in the middle of the war. In the eyes of many American officials, the threat from these Communist revolutionaries was even greater than the threat from the German military. Communist revolution, then, proved to be a powerful spur to the growth of the American intelligence industry. Communist movements have been a major target of U.S. intelligence ever since.

Following the war, the FBI took the lead in fighting what it saw as the Communist menace inside the United States. Under J. Edgar Hoover, who took control of the Bureau in 1924, the FBI became deeply involved in domestic spying on American radicals.

Thanks to the domestic Communist scare, the FBI

continued to prosper in the decade after the war. But the military agencies were not so lucky. They suffered major cutbacks in the general demobilization (disbanding) that came after the war. The need for foreign intelligence, which had been so clear during the war, was less obvious during the peace that followed.

It wasn't until World War II that a major new intelligence agency was founded. That new agency turned out to be very different from its forerunners. While they specialized primarily in the techniques of espionage and counterespionage, the new Office of Strategic Services (OSS) specialized in something else entirely—the daring and dangerous exploits of covert action.

3

COVERT ACTION IN WARTIME—THE OSS

Until World War II, no government agency was officially designated to carry out paramilitary covert actions. Covert activities of any kind were used rarely, and only when specific circumstances seemed to require them. Even then, they were used with reluctance.

Many officials were embarrassed by anything that smacked of secrecy or underhandedness. Some considered even the most common forms of espionage below their dignity. Even in 1929, not long after code-breaking had helped the United States win World War I, the secretary of state, Henry L. Stimson, could still protest that "Gentlemen do not read each other's mail." [1]

But, after the United States entered World War II—while Japan was overrunning the islands of the Pacific and the Nazis were overrunning Europe—the niceties of diplomatic behavior were suddenly less important. There was a rush to rebuild the American intelligence agencies and to establish new ones.

"WILD BILL"

The key figure in the rebuilding of American intelligence was William J. Donovan. [2] Although Donovan was a successful Wall Street lawyer, he was nothing like the image that job title suggests. Known as "Wild Bill" to his many admirers, Donovan had a dashing and flamboyant personality. An adventurer at heart, he'd ridden with General Black Jack Pershing's cavalry into Mexico to chase the bandit-revolutionary Pancho Villa in 1916. A few years later, he emerged from World War I with more medals than any other American soldier, including the Congressional Medal of Honor.

Donovan was a great believer in the value of intelligence. He'd dabbled in it himself, acting as a part-time agent of the British Secret Service on at least two trips to Europe. When a civil war broke out in Spain, Donovan went there to see for himself what was going on. When Italy invaded the African nation of Ethiopia, Donovan went there too.

A conservative Republican in his politics, Donovan was also a personal friend of the Democratic president, Franklin Roosevelt.[3] In 1940, the president sent Donovan on an intelligence mission to England. The armies of Nazi Germany were marching across Europe. They had already taken Czechoslovakia and Poland. Britain's turn seemed to be coming. Many U.S. officials, including the American ambassador in London, assumed America's closet ally was doomed, but Roosevelt wasn't so sure. He wanted another view—Donovan's view.

Donovan was sympathetic to Britain, and his trip did nothing to change his opinions. He was particularly impressed by his old employers, the British intelligence services. The British system was much more sophisticated and effective than America's disorganized collection of underfunded agencies.

Roosevelt followed Donovan's advice to help Britain. It was what he'd wanted to do anyway. He also followed Donovan's advice a year later, when Wild Bill asked him to establish a new American intelligence agency. Donovan made the request in a memo to the president on June 10, 1941. What America needed, he said, was "a central enemy intelligence organization which would collect . . . at home and abroad, pertinent information concerning potential enemies."[4]

America was not in the war yet, but both Roosevelt and Donovan knew that it soon would be. A month later, the president made Donovan head of the new agency, the Office of Co-ordinator of Information, or COI. Five months after that, Japanese planes attacked the American naval base at Pearl Harbor, Hawaii. America was in the war.

MOVING TOWARD COVERT ACTION

A year after it was founded, the COI was reorganized. Its key elements were shifted to a new agency, called the Office of Strategic Services, or OSS.[5] The OSS was officially placed under the authority of the Joint Chiefs of Staff, made up of the heads of the different military services. As a practical matter, however, the new agency was controlled by Wild Bill Donovan. He would shape it into the first real covert action agency in U.S. history.

Donovan's idea of what his new organization should be was based on the British secret services he admired. One of them, in particular, appealed to him because of its emphasis on action. It was the Special Operations Executive, or SOE. The SOE was more a paramilitary organization than an intelligence agency. It specialized in sabotage. Its main job in the war was to stir up trouble for the Germans in the countries they occupied.

SOE agents were trained in secret commando camps. They learned a wide range of violent arts— from a variety of methods for blowing up enemy bridges and rail lines to an even larger number of ways of killing people with their bare hands. They were then sent behind enemy lines, where they helped local resistance fighters do maximum damage to the hated Germans.[6]

This way of working attracted Donovan. In early 1942, he had established a Special Operations Branch within the COI.[7] The new department's responsibilities included communicating with and helping guerrillas (paramilitary forces), as well as carrying out some of the most active forms of espionage and counterespionage.[8] It became one of the main elements of the OSS when that agency was established a few months later.

It's not clear how far Donovan's superiors intended him to move into the cloak-and-dagger world. Donovan's memo, asking the president to establish a "central enemy intelligence organization" in the first place, had not mentioned covert action. Roosevelt's order officially establishing the OSS instructed it to "[c]ollect and analyze such strategic information as may be required [by] the Joint Chiefs of Staff." But it also authorized the OSS to [p]lan and operate such special services as may be directed by . . . the Joint Chiefs of Staff."[9]

The Joint Chiefs, in turn, issued a directive spelling out the functions of the OSS. They gave it two main responsibilities. One was to collect "such political, psychological, sociological, and economic information" as might be useful to the military services. The other was to plan, develop, coordinate, and carry out "psychological warfare."[10]

Apparently, the Joint Chiefs intended the OSS to spend most of its time pulling together information gathered by the military agencies. Donovan was more than willing to do this, but he had some other things in mind as well. In another memo to Roosevelt, he proposed "a guerrilla corps, independent and separate from the Army and Navy and imbued with a maximum of the offensive and

31

imaginative spirit. This force should, of course, be created along disciplined military lines, analogous to the British Commando principles. . . ."[11]

The OSS's intelligence role was limited by some of the military agencies' reluctance to share information with Donovan's group. The military old-timers were jealous of the new agency's central role. Some may have been personally jealous of Donovan himself. Finding its intelligence function hampered by this lack of cooperation, the OSS concentrated even more on its growing use of covert action. Although it continued to collect intelligence throughout the war, it came to see itself primarily as a secret paramilitary force.

THE OSS GOES TO WAR

Donovan believed that "intelligence, subversion, and psychological warfare could be . . . a critical spearhead of the war in Europe."[12] The sharp point at the tip of that spearhead would be the covert commandos of his OSS, working behind enemy lines. They operated over much of the globe, including Europe and Asia. The biggest exception was Latin America. Both U.S. intelligence and covert activities in Latin America were reserved for J. Edgar Hoover and his FBI.[13]

Many of the grandest schemes of the OSS never came off. There was a plan to kidnap and/or assassinate Adolf Hitler, for example.[14] There was another to flood enemy Italy with counterfeit money to destroy the value of the Italian currency.[15] But some of the OSS's more realistic schemes made real contributions to the Allied war effort.

One of the OSS's first covert actions took place in North Africa in 1942. At that time, the French colony was supposedly run by the Vichy government of France. In reality, however, Vichy was redundant a puppet of Germany, whose armies had conquered France two years before.

OSS agents began organizing espionage activities in North Africa, and soon involved themselves in military and political negotiations as well. OSS agents sought out French Army officials who resented the Germans and were willing to cooperate with the United States. When America's General Mark Clark made a submarine trip to North Africa to talk with one of the French officers, OSS agents helped arrange the top-secret meeting.[16] It was probably the first time that an American covert action agency was involved in secret negotiations with foreign military and political officials.

The main focus of OSS covert actions was in Europe. Small groups of agents called Jedburgh teams were smuggled into occupied countries. Most often, they would be dropped behind enemy lines by parachute in the total darkness of a moonless night, so that they could not be seen from the ground. Some of the agents were Americans who had joined the OSS for adventure or to help the war effort. Some were European refugees who had escaped from their homelands before the Nazis took over.

Jedburgh teams worked alongside the resistance fighters in Greece. They fought with the Italians undermining the Fascist government of Benito Mussolini, and with the fierce partisans led by Tito in Nazi-occupied Yugoslavia. By the time the Allied military forces launched the massive D-Day invasion of occupied France, the OSS had nearly 900 French and American agents waiting for them behind the German lines.[17]

Late in the war, the OSS organized the Norwegian Special Operations Group, or NORSO. It consisted of teams of Norwegian-Americans who were parachuted into German-occupied Norway. By that time, the Allies were attacking Germany itself, and 150,000 German soldiers were rushing home from

33

Finland to defend their country. To get there, they had to cross Norway. Led by an OSS major named William Colby, the NORSO teams disrupted the German troops' movements by sabotaging the railroad lines they were traveling over.

Only about half the NORSO commandos who were supposed to be dropped into Norway actually got there. Four of the eight planes carrying them either missed their targets or had to return to their base before they could drop their human cargo.

The agents who did make it to the ground in Norway faced many hardships, such as grueling cross-country treks on skis through freezing, blinding snowstorms. But they did manage to harass the German troops by blowing up several rail lines. And they had the satisfaction of still being there when Germany surrendered to the Allies in early May 1945.[18]

Typically, OSS agents in Europe took part in sabotage and subversion. They disrupted transportation and communications, blew up roads, bridges, and rail lines, and occasionally ambushed enemy troops. It was a deadly and merciless game the agents were playing, in which they often killed enemy soldiers and sometimes even assassinated suspected traitors. Often, innocent civilians would be killed along with the intended victims. When booby traps (hidden explosive devices) are set, it's not always possible to control who will get in the way of the explosion.

Even the agents' most successful actions sometimes resulted indirectly in the deaths of innocent people. The Germans had a policy of brutal retaliation. When OSS agents blew up a bridge or ambushed a truckload of German soldiers, the Nazis would kill innocent civilians to discourage more attacks.

OSS agents who were caught were usually killed themselves. Because they operated covertly, they were not protected by the laws governing the treatment of prisoners of war. Most often, they would be cruelly tortured before they were killed, to force them to betray their fellow agents and the members of the resistance.

BURMA

The OSS's most spectacular mission took place far from the freezing snows of Norway and the sophisticated cities of occupied Europe—in the sweltering jungles of Burma. That Southeast Asian colony of Britain had been invaded by the Japanese in 1942. The invasion had succeeded with the help of many Burmese citizens who wanted the British out of their country at almost any price.

Britain smarted at the loss of Burma. It wanted its colony back. Donovan's OSS decided to see what it could do. It turned out that it could do a lot.

Starting with about twenty agents, soon after the Japanese invasion, the OSS force working in Burma eventually grew to 500 strong.[19] Many of them were agents who had parachuted into Burmese jungles. Led by a young officer named Carl Eiffler, they made contact with Kachin tribesmen in the remote hill region of Burma. The Kachin were as eager to drive the Japanese out of their country as they had been to get rid of the British. Although the OSS was supposed to be helping win Burma back for Britain, many of the agents sympathized with the Burmese desire for independence. But whatever happened to Burma after the war, their job was to get the Japanese out.

They organized 10,000 of the Kachin into a covert army. They trained them in the tactics of

Agents of the Office of Strategic Services recruited Kachin tribesmen in Burma during World War II to help drive out the Japanese.

guerrilla warfare, provided them with weapons and other supplies, and turned them into a powerful and efficient military force.

The Kachin disrupted Japanese communications and transportation in Burma in much the same way the European resistance movements were disrupting the Nazis. But they did even more. Before the war was over, the Kachin had retaken some 15,000 square miles (39,000 sq km) of Burma from the Japanese.[20] And, when the Allies finally did attack Burma, the OSS-trained Kachin played a major part in the defeat of two key Japanese army divisions.[21] The Burmese operation was far and away the most successful covert operation of the war. It may even have been the most successful covert operation in history.

THE END OF THE WAR

Even before the war was over, Wild Bill Donovan was worried about the future of his agency in peacetime. He knew that once the Germans and the Japanese were defeated, the main reason the OSS had been established would be gone and the government and the public would want to get the war behind them. There would be strong political pressure to cut back the intelligence agencies, if not scrap them altogether.

Donovan was convinced that would be a mistake. As he saw it, there would be just as much need for his agency after the war as during it. Lacking a "central foreign intelligence agency" in the years leading up to World War II had left the United States weak and vulnerable. Raw information about the dangerous situation in Europe had been available. Bits and pieces of it had even been gathered by the existing U.S. intelligence agencies. But there had been no central agency to put all the bits and pieces together: to see the deadly dangers they represented and to warn the president and the Congress.

Besides, although the threat from the Nazis, the Fascists, and the Japanese might be gone, a new threat was growing in the world. That was the threat of international Communism, led by the Soviet Union. The United States must not be caught unprepared again. And it wouldn't be—not if Donovan had anything to say about it. Once again, Communism was about to provide the spur for a new period of growth in the intelligence community.

Donovan began pushing for a peacetime agency in 1944.[22] Whether it would be a continuation of the OSS or some new agency altogether, the organization he wanted would not replace the other intelligence agencies. Instead, it would embrace them. It would be a super agency, with overall responsibility for U.S. intelligence. It would be the one that put all the pieces together, that figured out what they meant, and that explained it all to the president.

The war in Europe ended in May 1945. The war in the Pacific ended the next August. Donovan had been right to worry. Peace did indeed spell the end of the OSS. But the end of the OSS did not mean the end of covert action as a tool of American foreign policy. It was only the beginning.

THE LEGACY OF THE OSS

What was the historic significance of the OSS? It was the first agency in U.S. history to have a truly central role in national intelligence. It was also the first agency that had specific authority to plan and carry out covert actions. But what did it accomplish with those powers?

38

Historians and other observers disagree about the importance of the OSS to the Allied victory in World War II. Most do agree that the intelligence collected by the OSS was of some real help to the Allied military effort. But there is much debate about the importance of the OSS's covert activities.

Supporters of covert action argue that the aid the OSS supplied to the European resistance movements helped them to harass and disrupt the enemy at key points during the war. They argue that the nearly 900 agents the OSS dropped into France were especially valuable at the time of the D-Day invasion, and they glory in the successes of the Kachin tribesmen in Burma. They point out that over half the American members of the Jedburgh teams in Europe received military decorations, and that the OSS unit responsible for the Burma operation received a special commendation of its own.[23]

But critics like Phillip Knightley, a journalist who specializes in intelligence matters, claim that these successes came at too high a cost. They point not just to the more than 400 OSS agents who were killed or injured in the war, but to the thousands of resistance fighters and innocent civilians killed in retaliation for OSS activities. Although Knightley admits that some OSS exploits involved acts of "enterprise, valour, and self-sacrifice of the highest order," he describes the OSS contribution to victory as "minimal."[24]

Despite these disagreements over the OSS's importance to the war effort, both critics and supporters agree on the lasting influence its example would have on American intelligence after the war.

The OSS had dramatically combined two very different functions: intelligence gathering and covert action, particularly paramilitary action. There would be an effort to separate those functions after the war, but it would fail. The example set by the OSS would be too strong.

When a new, larger, and much longer-lasting intelligence agency was founded a few years later, it was built in the image of the OSS. Even today, that agency, the CIA, remains the most enduring legacy of the OSS.

The influence of the wartime OSS on the peacetime CIA is reflected in the men selected to head the CIA over four decades. Four of the most powerful CIA directors have been men who served in the OSS: Allen Dulles (the CIA head from 1953 to 1961), Richard Helms (1966–72), William Colby (1973–76), and William Casey (1981–87). These men brought to the Agency the memory of William Donovan and his daring, can-do approach to problems. They also brought with them his belief in covert action as a way to solve them.

4

THE CIA

In his campaign for a super intelligence agency, Donovan had a powerful friend in Franklin Roosevelt. But he also had a powerful enemy in J. Edgar Hoover, the longtime head of the FBI. Hoover had never liked the OSS, or Donovan either. He was jealous of both of them.

In the 1930s, Hoover had tried to get control of worldwide U.S. espionage and counterespionage for his FBI. He didn't get it all, but he did get half the world. Roosevelt gave the FBI responsibility for counterespionage inside the United States, and for intelligence generally throughout the Western Hemisphere.[1] When the OSS came along, Hoover saw it as a threat to the FBI's power. And he saw Donovan as a threat to his own role as the most important figure in U.S. intelligence.

From the start, he treated the OSS as an enemy—not an enemy of the United States, but of the FBI. He had his agents infiltrate the OSS the way they infiltrated pro-Nazi political organizations and the American Communist Party.[2]

Hoover took his rivalry with Donovan so far that it actually endangered intelligence operations. On one occasion, the FBI discovered that OSS agents were burgling a foreign embassy in Washington, D.C., to find the key to an enemy code. Hoover had

*J. Edgar Hoover (left), who was
the longtime head of the FBI.*

his men set off a police siren outside the building to scare them off.[3]

Once the war was winding down and the struggle for control of peacetime intelligence was under way, Hoover knew that Wild Bill Donovan would be his main rival. He was determined to undermine him in every way he could.

The opportunity came when he got his hands on a memo Donovan had written to the president. In it, Donovan had set out his ideas for a "central intelligence service," directly responsible to the president. They were big ideas. The new agency would coordinate all the other government intelligence agencies. It would have the "final" authority to evaluate and disseminate intelligence to the other departments of government. In other words, it would be the one to decide which government officials found out what. What is more, it would also have the responsibility for "subversive operations abroad," that is, for covert action.[4]

The memo represented a direct threat to Hoover's role as the head of internal U.S. intelligence. He feared that if its suggestions were taken, the FBI would be turned into a mere department of the new agency. Hoover saw a chance to wreck Donovan's plan by using the memo itself. Properly presented, Hoover thought, the plan could be seen as a threat not only to the FBI but to the whole American system of government. If the memo were made public in the right way, the proposed agency could be painted as an attempt to establish a massive American secret police.

Hoover turned the memo over to a sympathetic reporter, Walter Trohan.[5] Trohan published it, describing the proposal as an effort to create "an all-powerful intelligence service to spy on the postwar world and pry into the lives of citizens at home . . . ."[6] The article set off a storm of controversy, both within the government and among the American people. Hoover had gotten off a devastating first strike in the propaganda war for the future of American intelligence.

But Donovan was also a veteran when it came to propaganda, and he had some powerful weapons of his own. The OSS had employed many journalists and writers, and he called on them to launch a massive counterattack.[7] Soon, a whole barrage of stories praising the exploits of the OSS began appearing in the press. They presented Donovan and his secret agency not as threats to American freedom but as its best defenders.

THE DEATH OF THE OSS

Donovan may or may not have eventually won the war for public opinion. But the final decision on the new agency wasn't up to the public; it was up to the president. And Franklin Roosevelt liked and trusted Wild Bill Donovan a lot more than he did J. Edgar Hoover.

The president approved Donovan's plan in a general way in April 1945. Unfortunately for Donovan, the approval was not a formal one. When Roosevelt died the next week, it counted for nothing. The decision would have to be made all over again by the new president, Harry Truman.

Truman was suspicious of the whole idea of a powerful national intelligence service, particularly one with both police powers and the potential for covert action. What is more, he was not fond of either Donovan or Hoover. Instead of deciding in favor of either of them, he decided against both. Neither would get control of a new peacetime intelligence agency. There would be no new agency.

Even worse, from Donovan's point of view, Truman signed an order dismantling the OSS once and for all on September 20, 1945. Some of the OSS's old jobs were given to other agencies (foreign espionage went to the War Department, and some other functions went to the Department of State), but the covert action branch was simply eliminated. Truman wanted no part of covert actions.

The only comfort Donovan could take from Truman's decision was that Hoover and the FBI got no part of his old agency. But, for the moment at least, Donovan's idea of a super agency was dead.

THE FIRST CENTRAL INTELLIGENCE AGENCY

It wasn't long before President Truman decided he needed a central intelligence agency after all. The United States' interests now extended to practically every corner of the world. That meant the United States' need for up-to-date information extended to every corner of the world as well. There was just too much information pouring in now, from too many places. There had to be some central organization to collect and analyze it, to make sense out of it all.

Early in 1946, the president established an agency to do just that. Called the Central Intelligence Group, or CIG, it was under the direct control of another new institution, the National Intelligence Authority (NIA). The NIA, which was made up of the secretaries of state, war, and navy, appointed the members of CIG. The head of CIG, known as the director of central intelligence, was appointed by the president himself.[8] His first choice for the job was a Navy rear admiral, Sidney Souers.

When asked at a news conference whether CIG was a "revival" of the OSS, Truman hotly denied it.[9] And, in fact, it wasn't. CIG was much smaller and less ambitious than the OSS had been. What is more, it had none of the independence the wartime agency had had. It didn't even have its own staff. The people who worked for CIG came from the various departments represented on the NIA.

Even more significantly, CIG had no budget of its own. Not only did it have to get its funds out of the budgets of the departments represented in the NIA, it also had to account to them for how it spent the money. This meant that it couldn't take on any major projects without getting permission—and money—from the NIA.

CIG was not authorized to undertake covert activities of any kind, not even with NIA permission. Truman may have changed his mind about the need for a central *intelligence* agency, but he hadn't changed his mind about covert action.

About a year later, Congress passed the National Security Act of 1947, completely reorganizing the nation's military forces. Along the way, it reorganzed the intelligence services as well. The National Intelligence Authority was replaced by a new body called the National Security Council, or NSC. The NSC was made up of the president and the vice president, the secretaries of defense and state, and the director of the Office of Emergency Preparedness. It was given responsibility for protecting the nation's security.

CIG itself was reorganized and renamed the Central Intelligence Agency, or CIA. The CIA was to be an independent government agency responsible directly to the National Security Council. That meant it was responsible to the president. Unlike CIG, the CIA had its own staff and budget. But it still did not have one important thing the OSS had had—the authority to carry out covert actions.[10] At least, that's what most observers—including the members of Congress who passed the National Security Act—assumed.

As it turned out, however, there was a clause in the National Security Act that was open to a different interpretation. It gave the CIA the power "to perform such other functions related to intelligence affecting the national security as the National Security Council may from time to time direct."[11]

The words seemed innocent enough. It was the kind of clause that lawmakers often put into bills. They are designed not to change or undermine the general intention of the bill, but only to eliminate unnecessary confusion and hesitation for the officials who have to carry those intentions out.

In the case of the National Security Act, there is no evidence that the intention of the bill was to give the CIA authority for covert actions. President Truman later specifically denied that he, for one, had intended any such thing when he signed it.[12] But the clause was there, and it wasn't long before it was used.

THE CIA BECOMES A COVERT ACTION AGENCY

In early 1948, the National Security Council faced a major foreign policy problem in Italy. The Italians were about to hold an election, and it seemed likely that the Italian Communist Party, backed by the Soviet Union, was going to do well. It might even do well enough to unseat Italy's pro-Western government, led by the Christian Democratic Party.

A Communist victory would be a major defeat for the United States. Europe was divided between the Western bloc, led by the United States, and the Communist or Eastern bloc, led by the Soviet Union. For a Western bloc country like Italy to move into the Soviet camp was unthinkable from the American standpoint.

The National Security Council decided that "Between now and the April elections in Italy, the United States should as a matter of priority immediately undertake further measures designed to prevent the Communists from winning participation in the government. . . ."[13]

But what "measures"? One obvious answer was to give help, and especially financial help, to the Christian Democrats. Money can make a big difference in an election, particularly a close election as the one in Italy was expected to be.

The trouble was that U.S. money could not be given openly. That would give the Communists a powerful election issue to use against the Christian Democrats. They could charge them with being a tool of the American government, a government that had recently defeated Italy in the war.

So the question for the NSC was how to funnel money and other support to the non-Communist parties in Italy without anyone finding out about it. There was no agency in the government that had both the ability and the legal authority to carry out that kind of covert action. Unless . . .

In desperation, Secretary of Defense James Forrestal went to the CIA. There was that little clause in the National Security Act, the one that gave the CIA the right "to perform such other functions . . . as the National Security Council may . . . direct." Now the NSC was ready to direct. And what it wanted was for the CIA to undertake a form of covert action.

There were doubts. After all, the "other functions" were supposed to be "related to intelligence affecting the national security." Did interfering in a foreign election fall into that category? And what about the intention of Congress when it passed the law? It hadn't really intended to authorize this kind

48

of activity. But all doubts were set aside when President Truman approved the plan.[14] His fear of a Communist victory overcame his dislike of covert action.

The CIA did funnel the money to the Christian Democrats and other non-Communist parties, and the Communists lost badly. Its very first covert action was a great success. Meanwhile, the president was changing his mind about covert action in general. On June 18, 1948, he signed a new National Security Council directive, NSC 10/2, establishing an organization called the Office of Special Projects and later called the Office of Policy Coordination, or OPC.[15] The new agency was directed to carry out "any covert activities" up to and including "subversion against hostile states . . . , assistance to underground resistance movements, guerrillas and refugee liberation groups, and support of indigenous anti-communist elements in threatened countries of the world."[16] Not long after, the OPC became a part of the CIA.

In order to understand why the United States got its first real peacetime covert action agency when it did, it is important to understand the temper of the times. In a sense, it wasn't really peacetime at all. In the view of the U.S. government, the "hot war" against Germany and Japan had been followed by a "cold war" against international Communism. And Communism was doubly dangerous because it combined the military strength of the Soviet Union with a powerful ideology, the Communist philosophy, that was very attractive to poor people in many countries of the world.

The president who followed Truman in office, Dwight Eisenhower, expressed the challenge this way: "We face a hostile ideology—global in scope, atheistic in character, ruthless in purpose, and insidious in method."[17] America's armed forces could be counted on to defeat the Soviet military if it ever came to that. But defeating the spread of Communist ideology required other weapons. That ideology—"global . . . atheistic . . . ruthless . . . and insidious"—was the enemy the CIA was designed to fight.

THE CLANDESTINE SERVICE

International Communism was a massive enemy, and the CIA soon became a massive organization. Just how big it actually is, there is no way to be sure. Like its budget, the true size of the CIA is a secret. It is possible that nobody knows just how big it is. According to ex-CIA official Victor Marchetti, not even the Agency itself knows how many employees it has. This is partly because so many thousands of people work for the CIA on a part-time, off-again, on-again basis and partly because the different branches of the CIA do not always tell one another what they are doing. But it is also because officials in the more secret departments of the organization are notoriously "sloppy" at keeping records. What is more, says Marchetti, CIA officials have always tended to understate the size of the Agency. As a rule of thumb, he suggests that the CIA is probably always two or three times as big as it seems to be.[18]

Writing in 1975, the ex-CIA agent Philip Agee claimed that the Agency then had 16,500 employees and a budget of around $750 million, not including "its mercenary armies or its commercial subsidiaries. Add them all together [and] the agency employs or subsidizes hundreds of thousands of people and spends billions every year."[19] And that was before a general increase in CIA activities that took place under Director William Casey in the 1980s.

50

Not all the resources of the CIA are devoted to covert activities. These days, in fact, only a small proportion are. The CIA is made up of several directorates. Most of these are so-called "open" directorates. Only one of the directorates is "closed," or secret: the Directorate of Operations, or, as it is known within the Agency, the Clandestine Service ("clandestine" means "secret"). The Clandestine Service is responsible for CIA espionage and counterespionage activities around the world. It is also responsible for "special operations," otherwise known as covert action.

THE COSTS OF COVERT ACTION

The role covert action has played in the activities of the CIA has varied widely over the years. Official figures are impossible to find, but it is generally admitted that covert activities hit an early peak in the 1950s. Tensions between the United States and the Communist nations were growing rapidly, and U.S. covert activities were growing even faster. In 1949, the covert operations budget of the CIA was said to be only $4.7 million. Within three years, it was $82 million.[20] And it continued to soar after that.

In recent decades, the proportion of the CIA's budget devoted to covert activities has been relatively low. Partly this is because some recent presidents, like Jimmy Carter, did not like using covert action as a tool of foreign policy. But mostly the lower proportions were due to increased spending on other things. High-technology espionage equipment—spy satellites, for example—are very expensive. And they've been taking a bigger and bigger slice of the CIA's budget. The slice of the pie for covert activities probably reached a low in the late 1970s and early 1980s. By the mid-1970s, for example, it had dropped to only 4 percent of the CIA's budget,[21] from a high of about 74 percent in 1952.[22]

The small percentage was misleading, however. The CIA's overall budget was many times larger than it had been in the fifties and sixties. Furthermore, some of the funds for covert operations didn't come from the CIA's budget at all; they came from other departments of the government. At least $40 million of the covert help the CIA sent to rebels in Afghanistan in the 1980s came from the Defense Department's budget.[23]

In any case, the proportion spent in covert actions rose again during the 1980s. By the middle of the decade, the CIA was probably spending at least $500 million of its own on covert activities. There is no telling how much more was coming from other sources.

Altogether, in its four decades, the CIA has launched thousands of covert operations. Most have been small, and not very significant, involving payments to foreign journalists or minor foreign officials in return for small favors. But some have been massive, up to and including several paramilitary actions launched against other countries.

These covert actions, large and small, have influenced foreign elections and helped to determine the outcome of foreign wars. They have helped to put friendly leaders in power in some countries and have removed hostile leaders in others.

The cost of these covert activities has been great, not only in money but also in human lives—some of them American lives. And there has been a high price paid in American prestige as well.

In the following chapters, we will look at several specific covert operations. We will examine some of covert action's proudest successes, and some of its biggest failures. We will see what they have cost the United States, and what the country has gotten in return.

5 CIA SUCCESSES

Every covert action is controversial. It would be hard to find any CIA operation that supporters of the Agency would not defend on some grounds or other. Likewise, it would be hard to find one that critics of covert action would not attack.

The operations discussed in this chapter are among those usually praised by the defenders of covert action. They are considered some of the best examples of what covert activities can accomplish. Most of them, as we will see, took place during the golden age of covert action in the 1950s. The CIA was young in those days. It almost seemed that it could not fail, as success followed success around the globe.

PICKING A PRESIDENT IN THE PHILIPPINES

In the 1950s, the United States was clearly the dominant power in the world. Unlike all the other major powers, it had come out of World War II with its industries undamaged. It had the strongest military and the largest and healthiest economy in the world. But, at the same time, it was faced with what it saw as an evil and immensely powerful enemy: international communism.

Communism was clearly on the march in the 1950s. The Soviet Union had already swallowed up Eastern Europe in the aftermath of World War II. And now Communist political parties were gaining ground in the free countries of Western Europe, while Communist-led revolutions were breaking out in many of the poor countries of the world.

One of the most disturbing Communist rebellions was in the Philippines. Made up of more than 7,000 islands in the Pacific Ocean, the Philippines had been a virtual colony of the United States for almost half a century.[1] The United States had granted the country its independence in 1946, but the ties between the two countries had remained strong.

Most importantly, from the American government's point of view, the United States had (and still has) two important military bases in the Philippines, the largest U.S. naval and air bases anywhere outside the Americas: Subic Bay Naval Base and Clark Air Force Base.[2]

There were other ties as well. Some of them were emotional. Americans and Filipinos had fought side by side to free the islands from Japanese occupation. Many Americans felt they had a personal stake in the welfare of their wartime ally. And America had an economic stake in the Philippines as well. Several American companies had important interests there and some Filipino-owned companies had business interests in the United States.

But the Philippines was a poor country. Most of what wealth there was, was in the hands of a relatively small group of landowners and businesspeople. Most ordinary Filipinos were desperately poor and therefore wide open to the Communists' argument that the country's wealth should be shared more evenly.

American economic help was vital to keeping the

struggling economy going. By 1952, direct U.S. aid added up to about 11 percent of the Philippine government's total income.[3] The United States provided other kinds of help as well. American political assistants gave regular advice to the U.S.-backed government of the president, Elpidio Quirino. American military officials advised the country's armed forces in their battle against the Hukbalahap Communist guerrillas. Even so, the Huks, as the rebels were called, were gaining ground. American officials blamed their success on the weakness and corruption of the Quirino government.

Although Quirino himself was probably honest, the election in which he'd won the presidency had been marred by widespread violence and fraud. Not very popular to begin with, Quirino's government became even less popular as time went on. And as the government's popularity dropped, the Huks' popularity grew.

American officials in the Philippines felt sure that social, political, and economic reforms would go a long way to satisfy the Filipino people and undercut the Communists. But the Quirino government seemed to be unable, or unwilling, to move ahead with reforms. The Americans became convinced that a dynamic Filipino politician named Ramon Magsaysay would do better.

The American ambassador and powerful U.S. Army officers used their influence to pressure Quirino to name Magsaysay as defense secretary. Because of the importance of American support to the Philippines, Quirino had little choice.

Magsaysay turned out to be a great success as defense secretary, and the military situation began improving. Before long, a U.S. Air Force colonel named Edward Lansdale was using sophisticated propaganda techniques to build up Magsaysay's image, both inside the Philippines and in the United States.

Supposedly assigned to public relations work for the U.S. military, Lansdale was a CIA man. In time, he would become a kind of legend: a larger-than-life symbol of the CIA's covert activities. Supporters of the CIA would hail him as one of its greatest heroes, a secret leader in the desperate struggle against Communism in Asia. Critics of the CIA would paint him as a villain—an uninvited "ugly American," clumsily butting into the political affairs of other countries.

His legend really began in the Philippines. There, in addition to his work for Magsaysay, he was in charge of the CIA's "psywar," or psychological warfare compaign. One of his schemes involved draining the blood out of a dead Huk through puncture wounds on his neck. This trick worked to convince the victim's superstitious comrades that he had been killed by a vampire instead of in battle. They ran away in terror.[4]

Lansdale's efforts to promote Magsaysay were less bloody. They were designed to groom him for the presidency of the Philippines. On American advice, Magsaysay shifted his political loyalties, leaving Quirino's Liberal Party and joining the opposition Nationalists. This made it possible for him to run against Quirino in the next election.

It's not clear just how far Lansdale went to assure that Magsaysay won the presidency. William Colby later wrote that Lansdale "identified Magsaysay as a decent and honest alternative" to Quirino, and proceeded to give him "imaginative advice" and "other forms of Agency help, to see him elected president."[5] He doesn't say what those "other forms of Agency help" were.

Among them, however, was more than just "imaginative" advice and clever public relations work. There was at least the offer of large amounts of money as well. In 1952, Lansdale took Magsaysay to the United States. While he was there, Pentagon officials offered Magsaysay $500,000. The money was supposedly offered for use in his battle against the Communists, but the U.S. officials made it clear that it would be given in secrecy. Magsaysay could use it any way he wanted to. He would never be asked what he had done with it. He later claimed that he had never used the money at all.[6]

Whether or not Magsaysay took the Pentagon's offer, there is no doubt a lot of American money flowed into his political campaign.[7] Most of it apparently came from ordinary citizens with business or emotional interests in the Philippines. But at least some of it was U.S. government money in disguise.

The offer of money to Magsaysay would turn out to be an unusual kind of interference in the political affairs of a friendly country. But it was only unusual because the offer was made by the Pentagon. In the future, it would be the CIA who would funnel most U.S. government funds to foreign politicians.

Even then, the CIA, in the person of Lansdale, was the agency in charge of the U.S. efforts to make Magsaysay president of the Philippines. He was successfully portraying Magsaysay as a dynamic and popular leader. It must have been easy for him. A man who could convince hardened Communist guerrillas that they were being stalked by a vampire probably had little trouble convincing ordinary voters to elect an attractive candidate.

On the surface, the CIA's campaign for Magsaysay seemed much like any other well-financed political campaign. What made it different was that it was directed by the CIA. A foreign government, the United States, was covertly pushing its own handpicked candidate for the presidency of the Philippines. Officially, the United States claimed "absolute impartiality" in the election.[8]

Just a few days before the 1953 election, U.S. Navy ships steamed into the harbor at Manila, the capital city of the Philippines. The Navy said the visit was a friendly courtesy call, but the Filipino Liberals who opposed Magsaysay took it as a threat. They feared that the United States was preparing a military coup d'etat (takeover) of the government if Magsaysay lost the election.

They may have been right. At least some of Magsaysay's Nationalist supporters *were* preparing a coup in case the Liberals stole the election.[9] And, if the U.S. ships were not there to back up the possible coup, their arrival was a remarkably clumsy coincidence.

As it turned out, it didn't matter anyway. The Liberals did not have to steal the election; Magsaysay won easily. Publicly, it was a proud moment for the young nation. Privately, it was an equally proud moment for the even younger CIA. The Agency had flexed its muscles again. It had helped defeat the Communists in an election in Italy, and now it had put its own candidate in as president of the Philippines. They were two brilliant examples of political covert actions at work.

As president, Magsaysay was everything the CIA had hoped he would be. He launched a program of reform that undercut the appeal of the Communist ideology and directed a military campaign that virtually ended the threat from the Huks. There is no telling what else he might have accomplished for his country if he hadn't been killed in an airplane crash only a few years later.

Even Joseph Smith, an ex–CIA official in the Far East who now has doubts about many of the Agency's other covert activities, still points to the Magsaysay operation with pride. It was, he says, "one time when the Agency was on the side of the angels."[10]

SAVING BRITISH OIL IN IRAN

Around the same time the CIA was helping choose a leader for the Philippines, it was taking sides in another power struggle thousands of miles away. Once again there were both political and economic reasons for its actions.

Oil is vital to a modern society, and most of the world's oil comes from the Middle East. A large proportion of that Middle Eastern oil comes from the country of Iran. In the early 1950s, Iranian oil was controlled by a single British firm, the Anglo-Iranian Oil Company, or AIOC.

Under a contract with the Iranian government, AIOC had exclusive rights to all the oil from southern Iran. It paid the government a fee. Then it drilled, refined, shipped, and sold the oil and kept the profits for itself. The profits were enormous. They came to ten times more than the amount AIOC paid to Iran for its oil.[11] Many Iranians protested that this was unfair, but the British insisted that a deal was a deal.

Like Britain itself, Iran was a constitutional monarchy. The head of the government was a monarch called a shah, but most real political power was in the hands of a parliament and a prime minister. In 1951, a new prime minister, Mohammad Mossadeq, came into office. He opposed the deal with the AIOC. Under a law that had been passed years before, the deal was up for review. Instead of just reviewing it, Mossadeq called for nationalizing the AIOC.

Britain appealed to its American ally for help. The flow of Iranian oil to Europe was threatened. The British suggested some kind of joint covert action to overthrow Mossadeq. First President Truman, and then President Eisenhower who succeeded him, hesitated.

By 1952, the situation was boiling down to a struggle for power between Mossadeq and the young Shah, Reza Pahlavi. Britain and the United States were pulling for the Shah. They felt sure they could deal with him about the oil. But Mossadeq was impossible. At one point, he even shut down the Iranian parliament.[12] The Shah ordered him to step down as prime minister, but Mossadeq refused, and there seemed to be nothing the Shah could do about it. He left his country and throne and went into exile in Rome.

President Eisenhower grew more and more worried as the crisis continued to build. Mossadeq's power seemed to be growing, and there was no sign of a settlement on the oil issue. Eisenhower feared that the Soviets might find a way to take advantage of the situation. He read in alarm the reports that the Iranian Communist party, the Tudeh, was staging large street demonstrations. Was Mossadeq himself a secret Communist? In 1953, Eisenhower finally told the CIA to go ahead with a plan to unseat Mossadeq.[13]

By that time, Mossadeq was moving to take personal control of the Iranian Army, which was under the command of the Shah. Control of the Army was crucial. The CIA sent Kim (Kermit) Roosevelt, a grandson of President Theodore Roosevelt, into Iran. The young Roosevelt had come up with the final plan to unseat Mossadeq, and he was the logical one to carry it out.

Roosevelt understood that the battle for power in Iran would be fought in the streets. In his own words, he "produced a mob" to counter the one the Tudeh already had demonstrating.[14] Working with only a handful of CIA agents—but with mil-

*The streets of Tehran during
the time of the ousting of
the prime minister of Iran.*

lions of U.S. dollars to spend—Roosevelt recruited thousands of demonstrators. In addition, he had U.S. officials in Iran supply pro-Shah army units with weapons to put down the Tudeh mobs and take Mossadeq himself prisoner.[15] The Shah returned to power.

In the eyes of the president, the CIA, and the British government, the covert action in Iran was a brilliant success. All the major goals of the operation were achieved within weeks of Kim Roosevelt's arrival in the country. Mossadeq was gone, and a new oil agreement was quickly negotiated. Both Eisenhower and Britain's prime minister, Winston Churchill, personally congratulated Roosevelt for his achievement.[16]

As an added bonus, Shah Reza Pahlavi was firmly established in power. He would stay there for a quarter of a century to come. Grateful for the help he'd received from the CIA, he would remain a strong ally of the United States throughout his reign.

THE INVASION-THAT-WASN'T-AN-INVASION IN GUATEMALA

Jacobo Arbenz Guzmán was elected president of Guatemala in 1951. Although his election went unnoticed by most Americans, it was viewed with annoyance by high U.S. government officials. Arbenz was a leftist. Although he was not a Communist himself, CIA analysts thought that the Communists might use his leftist policies to bring communism into Guatemala through the back door.

The thought of Guatemala's "going Communist" was frightening to U.S. officials. Located just below Mexico, little Guatemala was, as U.S. officials put it, in the United States' "backyard." It was unthinkable that such a close neighbor would ever "go Communist."

The CIA's fears were soon reinforced. The Arbenz government tried to buy weapons from the United States. The United States, which had refused to sell arms to the previous Guatemalan government as well, turned down the offer. When Guatemala tried to buy arms from other Western governments, the United States pressured them not to sell either. Unable to buy weapons anywhere else, Arbenz turned to the Soviet Union. Some U.S. officials took this as proof that Arbenz was willing to cooperate militarily with international communism.[17]

Another sign of Arbenz's leftist leanings was his nationalizing of American property in Guatemala. The property in question belonged to the United Fruit Company. United Fruit was taking advantage of the country's lush tropical climate, and its incredibly cheap labor, to grow bananas. Its plantations covered more than half a million acres, making the company the biggest landowner in Guatemala.[18]

Starting in 1953, Arbenz's government began to take control of the company's plantations and to give out parcels of the land to the peasants. The government paid for the land in government bonds, but gave the company no chance to turn down the sale.

United Fruit appealed to the United States to do something about this left-wing government that was taking away its property. The economic interests of United Fruit and the foreign policy interests of the United States were becoming confused. To many in Washington, Arbenz's seizing of United Fruit property proved he must be a Communist. In any case, the company's appeal fell on friendly ears.

The U.S. secretary of state was John Foster Dulles, who had once worked for United Fruit.[19] The job of getting rid of Arbenz was given to the CIA, which was headed by Dulles's brother, Allen. Both Dulles brothers were fiercely anti-Communist.

The CIA launched what amounted to a covert attack on the Arbenz government.[20] It was given the code name Operation Success. The attack had two main elements. One was a ragtag paramilitary force, and the other was a sophisticated propaganda effort. In an ordinary war, a government will mount a small propaganda effort to support a major military operation. But in Guatemala, the CIA did just the opposite. It mounted a small military force to support a major propaganda operation.

The CIA recruited a few hundred antigovernment Guatemalans and sent them to a training camp in nearby Honduras. There, the CIA began training them to invade Guatemala. They were led by Colonel Carlos Castillo Armas, who had been in exile from Guatemala since he'd failed to overthrow an earlier government some years before.

While this tiny invasion force was being prepared, the CIA set up a secret radio station to broadcast into Guatemala. Called Radio Liberation, it did its best to persuade Guatemalans that the Arbenz government was not only Communist but antidemocratic. The fact that Arbenz had been democratically elected, with more than 50 percent of the vote, was largely ignored.[21] The broadcasts were aimed particularly at the Guatemalan Army, which the CIA hoped would revolt against Arbenz.[22]

On June 18, 1954, the CIA's little army "invaded" Guatemala. Castillo Armas rode to war in an aging station wagon, while his 140 soldiers rode in old trucks.[23] None of them rode very far. A few miles inside the border they came to a stop. The bulk of the "invasion" would take place in the air—and on the airwaves. Radio Liberation and a few small CIA planes turned Armas's handful of troops into an unstoppable invasion force.

David Atlee Phillips, who ran Radio Liberation, later explained how his station gave Guatemalans the "impression" that a powerful invasion force had landed.[24] It announced, for example, that it could not confirm reports that as many as 5,000 people had been killed in a battle in some remote region. The station was telling the truth—in a sense. It couldn't confirm how many people had been killed. But that was because no one had been killed at all. There had been no battle, and no reports of a battle either. Radio Liberation had made the whole thing up. But Radio Liberation's listeners got the "impression" that there had been a great battle.

A further illusion of reality was given to the "invasion" by a series of air attacks, carried out by single-engine CIA planes, flown by American and Chinese pilots paid by the CIA.[25] They flew low, dropping hand grenades and sticks of dynamite on selected targets, giving an "impression" of a rebel air force on a bombing mission.

The great bluff worked beautifully. Facing an apparently massive invasion force, with only a disloyal Army to protect his government, Jacobo Arbenz Guzmán resigned.[26] Castillo Armas, the CIA's handpicked choice to lead Guatemala, took over. The United Fruit Company got back its land.[27] And, most important of all, the danger of a Communist takeover of Guatemala was ended.

If anything, President Eisenhower and the Dulles brothers were even more pleased with the operation in Guatemala than with the one that was set up in Iran. Years later, Allen Dulles would point to Guatemala as a prime example of a truly successful covert operation.

BLEEDING THE SOVIETS IN AFGHANISTAN

In the 1950s, it seemed that the CIA could do no wrong. Few Americans had any real idea of what the CIA actually did, but most thought well of the Agency. They had the "impression" that it was somehow helping to protect the United States from danger. As the ex–CIA director William Colby has written, "Even the occasional exposure of CIA failures did not substantially change this general picture. Charges of CIA responsibility for espionage and sabotage operations against China, Albania and Eastern Europe were passed off" as lies.[28] In those days, propaganda worked as well in the United States as it did in Guatemala.

In the 1960s and 1970s, however, covert successes were much harder to come by. What is more, the public "impression" of the CIA, and covert action in general, was rocked by a string of highly publicized disasters that began at the Bay of Pigs in Cuba in 1961 (see Chapter Six). It was not until the 1980s that covert action made a major comeback under President Ronald Reagan and his CIA director, William Casey. Perhaps their most notable success was in aiding the anti-Communist guerrillas in Afghanistan.

The Afghanistan operation actually began during the Carter administration, but it reached its peak under Reagan. One of the CIA's functions was to "create and exploit troublesome problems for International communism."[29] Afghanistan was that kind of problem for the Soviet Union, and the CIA rushed to exploit it.

In the late 1970s, the Communist government of President Hafizullah Amin of Afghanistan was under enormous pressure. It was being threatened from within by a violent feud with another Communist, but anti-Amin, faction. And it was being threatened from without by rebels who resented

66

William Casey was a director
of the CIA and the subject of
much controversy over what
he knew about the Iran-Contra
scandal. He took his secret,
if he had one, to his grave.

the government's heavy-handed control of their lives. The rebels were Muslims, and their hatred of the government was intensified by the Communist government's general hostility to religion.

In a covert action of its own, the Soviet secret police covert action agency KGB launched a paramilitary operation to bring order to the situation. Soviet paratroopers landed in Afghanistan. Supported by the anti-Amin Communists, they seized the capital city of Kabul. The president, his palace guard, and his family were all killed. A new Communist ruler, Babrak Karmal, was quickly installed as head of the government. He immediately "asked" for Soviet "assistance" to restore order, and the Soviets promptly responded by launching a virtual invasion of their neighbor.

The American president, Jimmy Carter, was outraged by the Soviet invasion. It was time, he decided, to teach the Soviets a lesson. Part of that lesson was public. He ordered an end to the shipments of American grain scheduled to go to the Soviet Union, and he refused to let American athletes participate in the 1980 Olympic Games in Moscow.

Another part of the lesson was secret. The president ordered a covert operation to support the rebels, who were now fighting both their own Communist government and the Soviets.

The covert operation was more than a simple knee-jerk reaction to the Soviet invasion. There was a strategy behind the president's plan. As Carter's chief foreign policy adviser, Zbigniew Brzezinski, put it, the aid to the rebels was designed to "bleed" the Soviets.[30]

Two decades before, the United States had gotten bogged down in a long, costly war to support an unpopular government in Vietnam. The Soviets had helped America's enemy in that war, and the fighting had gone on for years, draining America's economy, dividing its people, and sapping its will. And, in the end, the United States had lost.

This time, Carter realized, it could be the Soviets' turn to get bogged down in its own long and costly war to support an unpopular government. If so, the United States would do everything it could to see that it got good and stuck.

The operation was launched with lightning speed. "The first moment" after the invasion, as President Anwar Sadat of Egypt later reported, American planes were flying weapons to the rebels out of airports in Egypt.[31]

When Ronald Reagan took over the presidency in 1981, he restored the grain shipments to the Soviet Union. But his administration also increased the aid going to the rebels he called the "freedom fighters" in Afghanistan. In the mid-1980s, American aid climbed to as high as $500 million in a single year.[32]

Meanwhile, the Soviets were doing just what Carter and Brzezinski had hoped they would do. They were getting mired deeper and deeper in the muck of a guerrilla war they could not win. And, the deeper the Soviets sank, the more help the United States gave the rebels.

The United States was not alone in supplying the rebels. Egypt, Pakistan, and Saudi Arabia were some of the other countries that helped. But the United States, through the CIA, was far and away the most important supplier of weapons for the rebels. Among the advanced weapons it provided were stinger missiles, which allowed the rebels to shoot Soviet warplanes out of the sky.

By the late 1980s, it was clear that the rebels were winning their battle against the Soviets. The Soviet Union's will to fight was being drained every bit as dry as America's had been in Vietnam. In 1987, the Soviet government announced that it would pull out of Afghanistan. The last Soviet

Soviet troops began withdrawing from Afghanistan in spring 1988. The CIA aided the Afghan resistance, which had fought against the Soviets. Although it is still not clear which side will come out ahead in Afghanistan, Soviet soldiers can probably thank the CIA for playing an indirect role in their government's decision to withdraw.

troops actually left the country in February 1989. In the decade they had spent there, the Soviets had lost at least 15,000 lives and suffered 35,000 other casualties.[33]

The CIA had some reason to be pleased with its ten-year covert operation. It had been expensive, but only in terms of money. No American troops had been sent into a single battle. No American soldiers had been lost. There had not even been a direct confrontation between the United States and the Soviet Union. And yet, thanks to covert action, the United States had played a part in handing the Soviets the first loss of a war they had ever suffered.[34] Doubts about the real value of what had been accomplished would only come later.

6

COVERT FAILURES

The actions discussed in this chapter are among the ones most often criticized by opponents of covert activities. They argue that these actions are examples of the dangers of a government's trying to do in secret what it is unwilling to do publicly.

THE BAY OF PIGS

In 1959, a revolution led by Fidel Castro overthrew the government of Fulgencio Batista in Cuba. Batista had been a dictator, but one who was friendly to the United States. It soon became clear that Castro would be a dictator as well, but he would not be friendly. Worse, he seemed to be a Communist.

The United States had a deep interest in Cuba's future. The small island was only about 90 miles off the southern coast of Florida. A lot of American money was invested in the country, and it was a popular vacation spot for American tourists. What is more, the United States had a naval base on one end of the island at Guantanamo Bay.

A Communist government in Cuba was unacceptable to President Dwight Eisenhower—particularly one that seemed determined to have close relations with the Soviet Union and to spread its brand of Communist revolution to the other countries of Latin America.

When Castro nationalized about $1 billion worth of property owned by U.S. citizens in Cuba, the United States broke off diplomatic relations with his government. Publicly, the American government protested Castro's actions. Privately, Eisenhower instructed the CIA to find a way to do something about the troublesome Cuban dictator.

In 1960, the CIA came up with a plan for an invasion of Cuba.[1] The invasion would not be carried out by Americans, but by anti-Castro Cubans. There were many of these exiles living in and around Miami, Florida. They dreamed of returning someday to liberate their beloved homeland. The CIA would give them their chance.

The plan combined elements from covert actions that had worked before. Its first stage was similar to that of Operation Success. Only this time, instead of training Guatemalan exiles in secret camps in Honduras, the CIA trained Cuban exiles in camps in Guatemala.

The second part of the plan was similar to the Jedburgh-team operations the OSS had carried out in Europe. Teams of commando-trained exiles would sneak into Cuba and organize the local resistance to Castro. Later on, a small invasion force would land on the island. Joining forces with the resistance, it would spark a general uprising against Castro.

The rebellion would be led by the CIA-trained invaders, who would direct it from hideouts in Cuba's rugged mountains. In that, they would follow the example of Castro, who had conducted his own revolution from those same hills. In the meantime, the CIA would launch a massive propaganda campaign against Castro, undermining his support.

That was the original plan, but as time went on, the plan began to change. By late 1960, the CIA had concluded that it would be impossible to build an effective resistance movement inside Cuba. There was simply not enough organized opposition inside the country. Because of this, the plan for landing small paramilitary groups in Cuba became a plan for a regular military-style invasion of the island. Instead of a handful of guerrillas, an invading force of 800 or 900 soldiers was to land near the Cuban town of Trinidad.[2]

The invasion would be supported by air strikes. Sixteen CIA-supplied B-26 bombers, flown by CIA-trained pilots, would hit Cuban airfields, wiping out the entire Cuban Air Force before it could leave the ground.[3] The sneak attack would prevent Cuban fighter planes from strafing the invasion force from the air.

The actual invasion, of course, could not be kept secret. The secret would be the CIA's and the U.S. government's role in the invasion. The plan called for the whole thing to look like the work of anti-Communist Cuban exiles, valiantly fighting to take back their country from a Soviet-backed dictator.

President Eisenhower had been kept informed of the plan as it developed. He approved the early stages of the plan in March 1960, and authorized several million dollars for it the following August.[4] But when the time came for the invasion to actually be launched, Eisenhower was no longer president. He had been replaced by John Kennedy.

Kennedy was not enthusiastic about the invasion. He wanted Castro out as much as Eisenhower had, but he wasn't sure the invasion could succeed. Even if it did, he doubted that the U.S. involvement could be kept secret. If the truth came out, it could harm the U.S. image abroad. Governments are not supposed to take part in overthrowing governments with whom they are not at war.

What is more, the United States had signed a 1937 treaty agreeing that it would not interfere in the internal affairs of any Latin American country.

But the CIA director, Allen Dulles, assured him that the plan could succeed. And besides, the United States was committed. The Cuban exiles of Brigade 2506 had been training hard for a year. They were counting on the CIA and the American government. Would Kennedy break the word of the United States government? He would not. The president okayed the invasion.

He and his advisers did, however, make two major changes in the CIA's plan, both of which were later criticized by those who blamed Kennedy for the disaster that followed. The administration was not happy with Trinidad as the place for the invasion. It was too heavily populated. The CIA was told to come up with another site. It chose a beach on the southern shore of Cuba known as the Bay of Pigs.[5]

The final CIA plan called for two air strikes. Kennedy authorized the first strike, which destroyed roughly half the Cuban Air Force two days before the invasion. But at the last minute he called off the second strike, which might have destroyed the rest of it.[6]

On April 17, 1961, the CIA and the U.S. Navy put 1,400 men of Brigade 2506 ashore at the Bay of Pigs. They were discovered almost immediately, and a battle followed. It began badly for the invaders and got steadily worse. The remaining planes of the Cuban Air Force—those which had survived the air strike—took to the air. One of them managed to sink the ship that was waiting offshore with the invaders' supply of extra ammunition.[7] It quickly became clear that the invaders were losing the battle.

When it was already too late to do much good, the president gave in and authorized another air

*Allen Dulles and John F. Kennedy
(left), when the latter was still
a presidential nominee. Later the
two would plan what would turn out
to be the botched invasion of Cuba
at the Bay of Pigs.*

strike, as well as a small amount of fighter support for the B-26s. Bitter American CIA agents, who could not believe how little support their government was giving the invaders, flew the planes themselves. They wanted to do what they could for the Cuban exiles, who had trusted them. Several of the planes were shot out of the sky.

Losing the battle was bad enough, but there would be no comeback from this loss, no war to win. Far from rising up against Castro, most of the Cuban public reacted with anger to the invasion of their country.

For the invaders, even a retreat into the mountains was impossible. Unlike the first site, the Bay of Pigs was far away from the mountains. With the Cuban Army in front of them, the sea behind them, and Cuban planes raining fire overhead, the invaders had nowhere to run. On Tuesday afternoon, the roughly 1,200 of them who were still alive surrendered; 114 had died on the beach.

The Bay of Pigs was the first great public failure of American covert action, and it was an extremely costly one. It was most costly of all for the men who went ashore at the Bay of Pigs.

Eventually, the captives were deported to the United States in return for the payment of $53 million in farm machinery and other ransom to the Cuban government. Officially, the money came from private sources, not from the U.S. Treasury. But the government was clearly behind the ransom effort, which was organized by President Kennedy's brother Robert.[8] For the anti-Castro Cubans, it was a sad blow to their romantic dream of returning to free their native country from Communist oppression. Three decades later, that dream is still alive. A new version of Brigade 2506 is in guerrilla training in the Florida wilderness today.[9]

The failure was also costly to the U.S. govern-

*An American plane wrecked
during the ill-fated invasion
at the Bay of Pigs.*

ment. Despite a State Department effort to deny it,[10] the U.S. role in the invasion was obvious to everyone. President Kennedy himself publicly took responsibility for the disaster. It was a humiliating defeat for the United States. Tiny Cuba had beaten off an invasion planned and supported by the strongest country in the world. And it had done it in just a couple of days.

It wasn't only the military prestige of the United States that suffered. Its moral prestige suffered as well. The United States was loudly condemned around the world. The condemnations came not just from Communist countries, but from many neutral and even friendly countries, including many anti-Communist countries in Latin America.[11]

The failure was also costly to the prestige of the CIA. The public image of the CIA—and of covert action in general—was badly damaged. "Indeed," says William Colby, "it is not too much to say that, more than any other single event, it was the abortive Cuban invasion, with all the attendant brouhaha in the United Nations and elsewhere, that imprinted the initials CIA into the general public's consciousness. And, what's more, it imprinted them in the most negative way possible. . . ."[12]

OPERATION MONGOOSE

President Kennedy and the CIA did not give up their desire to unseat Fidel Castro after the Bay of Pigs. If anything, they became more determined than ever. Directed by Kennedy to "get rid of" Castro, the CIA launched a new operation against him in November 1961.

Called Operation Mongoose, its purpose was to promote an "open revolt and overthrow of the Cuban regime." At the time it was begun, it was hoped that this revolt might come about within a year.[13]

The method to be used to encourage the revolt was the destruction of the Cuban economy. When things got bad enough, the CIA reasoned, the people would realize that Communism had failed. They would then be ripe for a revolution to overthrow Castro and return capitalism to Cuba.

Publicly, the United States refused to trade with Cuba and encouraged its allies to do the same. Cuba was a small agricultural country. It depended on its exports of sugar and tobacco. By starving Cuba of Western markets for its crops, the United States hoped to dry up the flow of foreign money into Cuba. That would make it hard for Cuba to purchase the machinery and consumer goods it needed from abroad.

Meanwhile, Operation Mongoose set out to ruin the economy in more direct ways. Headed by one of the Agency's most legendary figures, Edward Lansdale, and supervised by another, Theodore Shackley, it was the largest covert operation yet. Although the CIA was forbidden to do business inside the United States, Mongoose was operated from a building on the campus of the University of Florida in Miami.[14]

Once again, the CIA turned to anti-Castro exiles to carry out its plans. Directed by the CIA, they carried out hundreds of sabotage missions against Castro. Using small boats to smuggle weapons and guerrilla commandos onto the island, they poisoned or set fire to sugar fields, blew up oil refineries, and even carried out guerrilla attacks on military targets inside Cuba.

The CIA's assault on Castro included more than economic sabotage. There were also at least eight different assassination attempts against Castro himself, as well as several efforts to discredit the Cuban leader.[15]

The most inventive was a plot to drug him during one of the many long speeches he often gave

80

over Cuban television. CIA agents planned to give Castro a secret dose of the drug LSD just before or during one of these televised talks.[16] LSD causes hallucinations and odd behavior. It gives the drugged person the illusion of seeing strange sights and feeling strange sensations. The plotters hoped the drug would cause Castro to exhibit "crazy" behavior that would embarrass him in front of the Cuban TV audience. But the plan never came off.

Although it was the most massive CIA operation in history up to that time, Operation Mongoose failed. Neither the personal attacks nor the economic warfare managed to "get rid of Castro." Although the CIA-sponsored sabotage did great damage to the Cuban economy, it never completely destroyed it. Extensive economic aid from the Soviet Union managed to prop up the country's finances.

Politically, the operation was an even greater failure. There was no revolution in Cuba. If anything, the opportunity to fend off the attacks from the United States made Castro more popular than he had been before. He was a David fighting the U.S. Goliath—and winning.

Far from driving Communism out of Cuba, the secret war cemented the ties between Cuba and the Communist bloc. By making Cuba economically dependent on the Soviet Union, it drove the two countries closer together politically as well.

Operation Mongoose died out in 1963 sometime after the Cuban missile crisis. Some people who knew about the CIA attempts to kill Castro wondered if the killing of Kennedy had been an act of revenge on the part of the Cubans. Among them may have been Kennedy's successor, President Lyndon Johnson, who ordered the assassination attempts on Castro stopped.[17]

Operation Mongoose marked the second failure of a major covert action against Cuba. But it was, at least, a quieter failure than the Bay of Pigs had been. Although Castro was obviously aware of what the CIA had been doing in Operation Mongoose, most of the American public was not.

THE SECRET WAR IN LAOS

At the time of the Bay of Pigs invasion, the United States was already becoming involved in a growing war in Southeast Asia. That involvement would go on well into the 1970s. Before it was over, it would cost the United States many billions of dollars and over 50,000 American lives. (It would cost the countries of Southeast Asia even more.) And it would result in what most historians consider the worst military and foreign policy defeat in American history.

Most of the public's attention during that time was focused on South Vietnam, the country where the majority of U.S. combat troops were fighting. But the so-called Vietnam War actually covered a much wider area, spilling over into the neighboring countries of Laos, Cambodia, and Thailand as well. And much of the U.S. involvement in the war was covert, going on largely unknown to the American public and even to Congress.

The most controversial of the CIA activities in Vietnam was Operation Phoenix. The operation was led by William Colby, who later was named CIA director. Its job was to find and destroy local Communist leaders in the towns and villages of South Vietnam, and it did its job with merciless brutality. Critics of Phoenix consider it little more than a vast "death squad" operation designed to intimidate opposition to the anti-Communist government of South Vietnam. Defenders argue that it was simply a military intelligence operation designed to identify members of a particularly sneaky enemy in wartime. Officially, the U.S. government admits that Operation Phoenix killed some 21,000 civilians. Most of them, it insists, were Communist rebels. Critics of the CIA, however, claim that at least 40,000 civilians were killed.[18]

There is not space to go into the entire history of U.S. covert actions in Southeast Asia in detail, but we will examine one small part of it—the "secret war" the CIA carried out in Laos. The failure of that war was only a part of the greater failure of American military and foreign policy in Southeast Asia as a whole, but it has a special place in the story of covert action. Covert activities were essential to U.S. strategy throughout Southeast Asia, but in Laos, covert action was the heart and soul of that strategy.

In Laos, as Victor Marchetti has written, "the CIA actually led the rest of the U.S. government— at the White House's order—into a massive American commitment."[19] As we shall see, the debt built up by that commitment is still being paid inside the United States today.

In the early 1960s, various right-wing, left-wing, and neutralist forces were battling for control of Laos. The left-wing Pathet Lao guerrillas were supported by the Soviet Union and by several thousand soldiers from Laos's Communist neighbor, North Vietnam. Fearing a Communist takeover of Laos, the United States was giving military help to the right-wing forces.

In 1962, the United States, the Soviet Union, and twelve other nations met in Geneva, Switzerland, and worked out a political settlement for Laos. A coalition government was formed, made up of representatives of all sides.

It wasn't long, however, before right-wing leaders made attempts to take over the country. Some joined forces with neutralists to establish what amounted to a right-wing regime, technically under the largely powerless king of Laos. With North Vietnamese help, the Pathet Lao went to war against the new government.

One part of the Geneva Agreement called for all foreign military forces—North Vietnamese *and* Western—to leave Laos. Neither the North Vietnamese nor the Americans really honored their promise. Only 40 of the 7,000 North Vietnamese in Laos left.[20] (The 7,000 were eventually joined by over 60,000 more.) And, although the United States did not send regular troops into Laos at that time, it did send the CIA.

As the ex–CIA agent Harry Rositzke described the CIA's mission in Laos, it was to build "a secret army, designed to evade the Geneva Agreement. . . ."[21] Pretending to honor the Agreement, the CIA operated out of Thailand instead of Laos. But that was only a technicality. CIA agents traveled to and from Laos whenever they wanted to, using the CIA's own airline, Air America, as a kind of commuter shuttle from Thailand.[22]

The operation began small. In the words of Ray S. Cline, a onetime deputy director of the CIA, "a few paramilitary case officers" were sent into Laos "to establish small teams of [Laotian Hmong] to harass Vietnamese infiltrators and collect intelligence on their relationship with the local Pathet Lao insurgents. It took guns and guts and careful direction to do this. This initial effort was so successful and so inexpensive that the program expanded from a few hundred skilled and loyal troops to 30 or 40 thousand in the end."[23]

The CIA worked largely through the so-called l'Armée Clandestine (French for "Secret Army"). Although technically a part of the Royal Laotian Armed Forces, l'Armée Clandestine (the *l'* means "the") was really a separate force under the personal command of a dynamic Royal Laotian Air

*Laotians are shown being evacuated
from an air base in Laos in 1970.
In the 1960s and early 1970s,
the CIA recruited Laotians
of the Hmong tribe to fight
Laotian and North Vietnamese
Communist soldiers in Laos.*

Force officer named Vang Pao. It was made up of pro-Western Laotians of the Hmong (or Meo) tribe, who lived in the Laotian highlands. William Colby, who was then the chief of the CIA's Far East operations, had a high opinion of the Hmong, whom he referred to as "our friends in the mountains."[24] In that, he was typical of most of the Americans who dealt with them.

U.S. officials considered the members of l'Armée Clandestine to be volunteer freedom fighters battling for the liberty of their homeland. The ex–CIA agent Victor Marchetti called them "the CIA's private army."[25] Whatever they were called, Colby found them a much better fighting force than the rest of the Royal Laotian Army put together. They numbered 40,000 at the very most. Even then, only 15,000 or so were actually trained as guerrilla fighters.[26] Yet they fought for years, not only against the Pathet Lao but against the 70,000 North Vietnamese soldiers in Laos as well.[27]

According to Rositzke, among others, the CIA "carried the main burden" of recruiting, arming, and supplying the Hmong.[28] In addition to the military campaign, the CIA opened propaganda and political action campaigns to win the people of Laos away from the Pathet Lao. Among other things, it established its own radio station in Thailand to broadcast propaganda into Laos.

The CIA was not alone. As in other political operations elsewhere in the world, the Agency was greatly helped by the Agency for International Development (AID), the State Department, and other U.S. agencies operating in Southeast Asia. AID, in particular, operated a number of economic development projects, and gave food and medical and relief assistance to refugees fleeing the fighting.[29]

The secret operation was "blown" (which is spy talk for "revealed") by news stories in 1969. Many members of Congress were outraged. The CIA had been, in effect, fighting a secret war in Laos for nearly a decade and had never told Congress about it. The angry Congress quickly passed the Cooper-Church Amendment, which forbade the president to send "American ground combat troops" into either Laos or Thailand.[30]

U.S. backing of l'Armée Clandestine, including air support for Vang Pao's declining forces, continued into the 1970s. It finally ended, along with the rest of the U.S. military effort in Southeast Asia, in 1973.

Many people in the CIA were proud of what the Agency had accomplished. It had run a virtual war in Laos, and it had done it with an amazingly small investment of American resources. For more than a decade, the Hmong had held off both the Pathet Lao and the North Vietnamese.

And yet, say the critics, despite the efficiency of the CIA and the bravery and skill of the Hmong, the secret operation in Laos turned out to be a failure. The CIA and l'Armée Clandestine lost the war. The Communist-led People's Democratic Republic of Laos was officially proclaimed in 1975.

The effects of the failure in Laos are still being felt—and not just in Laos, but in Thailand and the United States. Because of the collapse of the "secret war," huge numbers of the Hmong were forced into disease-ridden refugee camps in Thailand. Nearly two decades later, tens of thousands of them are still there. Children who were born in the camps are now having children of their own, to be raised in conditions of miserable poverty.

The United States government, which enlisted the Hmong in its battle in Laos, has recognized a moral obligation to them. It is still trying to pay off its debt by allowing at least some of the refugees into the United States. So far, about 100,000 of them have arrived, and more are coming. Roughly half live in California,[31] and many others

*After the United States pulled
its troops out of Southeast
Asia, many Hmong were relocated
to the United States. The
family shown here is at a
refugee camp in Washington State.*

in small communities in the Midwest. The rest are scattered about the country.

In this country, they have the chance for a better economic future than they would have in the camps. But they face a strange and often hostile culture as well, along with the bigotry, bitterness, and resentment of many of their American neighbors.

Many of the Hmong, especially those who came here as young children, are adjusting well. They are likely to become happy and successful citizens of their new country. Others, particularly members of the older generation that fought for the CIA in Laos, are finding it much harder to adjust. Thousands of them live isolated lives—bewildered and hopeless in a society they don't understand, and that doesn't understand them. All of this, critics argue, has to be figured in when counting the cost of the covert action in Laos.

THE RESCUE THAT FAILED

A past covert action success came back to haunt the United States in the late 1970s. The Shah, whom the CIA had put in power in Iran in the 1950s, had proved to be an unpopular ruler. The Shah tried to force many elements of modern Western culture on his very Middle Eastern country. This was resented by many of the people, who were very conservative in their social and religious attitudes. When the people protested the Shah's policies, his secret police, the Savak, brutally crushed the protests. This, in turn, led to more resentment. By the late 1970s, things were coming to a head.

The CIA, and therefore the United States government, misunderstood what was happening in Iran. It thought the Shah was firmly in control. As a result of this misreading of the situation, it strongly supported him. When the Shah was overthrown in a revolution headed by the religious leader the Ayatollah Khomeini, the anger of many Iranians focused on the United States. America, they knew, had put the Shah in power in the first place. It had given him the weapons he had used to crush their protests. Many Iranians believed the CIA had even trained the Savak in the techniques of interrogation and torture.

In November 1979, a mob of angry Iranian students stormed the U.S. embassy in the city of Tehran and took the Americans there hostage. The U.S. government appealed to the Iranian government to make the students release them. After some delay, however, it decided to allow the students to keep the hostages. Some of the prisoners were later released, but by April 1980, more than fifty Americans were still being held in one or more secret locations in Tehran.

President Jimmy Carter was under enormous political pressure to get them free. A special nightly television news show had been created just to deal with the hostage crisis.[32] Every day, it and the other news media spotlighted the plight of the hostages. It was not, the media kept saying, just the Americans in Tehran who were being held hostage. It was America itself. Many Americans felt humiliated that what they thought of as a "little" country like Iran could hold Americans hostage. Why couldn't the mighty United States do something about it?

President Carter tried. When negotiations brought no progress, he and his advisers searched desperately for another alternative. Through the good intelligence work of the CIA, they found out where the hostages were being held. A plan was devised to rescue them.

The rescue operation would have to be prepared and carried out in secrecy. If the people who held the hostages found out about it, they would move

90

A portrait of the Ayatollah Khomeini
hangs from the roof inside
the compound of the American embassy
after it was stormed in
1979 by Iranian students.

the hostages, if not kill them. Instead of turning to the CIA for the covert mission, Carter decided to use a special military commando unit called the Delta Force.

The Force had recently been established as a special unit to fight terrorists. Its 800 members had been handpicked for the job from the special operations units of the U.S. Army, Air Force, and Navy. They were specifically trained to carry out secret commando missions. It seemed to be just the group that was needed for the daring rescue attempt.

It would be a difficult mission with very special requirements. Key elements of the mission were helicopters that could land and take off inside a city. But helicopters had a limited flying range, and Tehran was a long way from any U.S military base from which they could take off. It was decided that the mission would have to be carried out in stages. The copters would have to be refueled on the way. A rendezvous (meeting) with fuel-carrying planes was set up at an isolated spot in the Iranian desert.

Eight helicopters took off on the rescue mission. Three of them had mechanical troubles and had to return to base. The other five continued to the rendezvous in the desert. There, the plan disintegrated in disaster. Somehow or other, one of the helicopters smashed into a transport plane on the ground, and eight of the commandos were killed. There were no longer enough people, or enough helicopters, to carry out the mission.

The Delta Force survivors returned to their base, never having reached Tehran. President Carter was forced to go on television to announce the tragic failure of a secret mission to rescue the hostages. That failure was all the more embarrassing because it had not been brought about by the Iranians. The rescue force had destroyed itself.

*Some of the debris from the
crash of one of the helicopters
in the Delta Force mission
whose goal was to rescue American
hostages in Iran. Note the
charred helmet in the foreground.
Eight American commandos were
killed in the ill-fated mission.*

The failure of the covert mission had to be made public because of the wreckage of the helicopter. It, and the bodies of the dead commandos, had to be left behind in the desert. The Iranians soon found the helicopter and triumphantly broadcast pictures of the remains of the secret mission to the world.

Although the rescue mission was much smaller than the other covert action failures discussed in this chapter, it had an enormous impact. As a result of it, many Americans felt more humiliated than ever. Jimmy Carter lost the presidency to Ronald Reagan in the next election. The disaster in the desert may well have sealed the doom of the Carter presidency.

7
QUESTIONS AND CONTROVERSIES

As Republican Senator Orrin Hatch of Utah has pointed out: "It is the nature of covert actions to be controversial."[1] There are many, including Hatch and most recent American presidents, who believe that covert action is a vital tool of American foreign policy. They are convinced that it is often necessary to use that tool if the peace and security of the United States are to be protected in a dangerous world.

But there are others, including many scholars and members of Congress, who believe that most covert actions are unnecessary, immoral, and dangerous. Although covert operations may sometimes prove useful, they are more often misguided and even counterproductive. And there are still others who believe that the whole idea of the government acting in secret runs against the basic principles of American democracy.

Both some of the strongest supporters and some of the strongest critics of covert action come from the ranks of ex–CIA agents and officers. The majority of these ex–covert operators support its continued use.[2] Some, like Harry Rositzke and Ray Cline, consider covert activities valuable in some circumstances but feel that they have been over-

95

used. Some, like Philip Agee and Victor Marchetti, argue that covert paramilitary actions, at least, should be ended altogether. "As for the CIA's paramilitary tasks," Marchetti has written, "they have no place in a democratic society."[3]

Is covert action really as vital to our national security as its supporters believe? Is it really as dangerous as its critics charge? Does it defend the American democratic system, or undermine it? And, however valuable, is it possible to keep it under control?

IS COVERT ACTION NECESSARY?

Is there any reason for our government to conduct covert activities at all? Can covert action accomplish anything that couldn't be accomplished just as well some other way? The supporters of covert action would say yes. They believe the ability to act in secret gives the United States something no other strategy can offer. In the words of the ex–CIA agent Theodore Shackley, it provides a needed "third option."[4] That is, it gives the government an alternative to either declaring war or doing nothing.

The United States was faced with just that kind of choice when the Soviet Union invaded Afghanistan. Without the possibility of covert action, supporters argue, it would have had to accept the Soviet invasion, or else send American troops into Afghanistan to drive the Soviets out.

Neither alternative was attractive. If the United States had accepted the Soviets' action, it would have invited them to invade other countries, safe in the knowledge that the Americans would do nothing about it. Sending American troops, on the other hand, could have been disastrous. Besides meaning the loss of many soldiers' lives, it might have angered the Afghans themselves. They didn't want American troops on their soil any more than they wanted the Soviets there. Even worse, it might have led to a wider conflict between the superpowers—and ultimately, perhaps, to nuclear war. Only the "third option," that of covertly helping the Afghan rebels, allowed the United States to combat the Soviet invasion without going to war itself.

Critics argue that this covert "third option" is unnecessary. There are many direct and open ways for the United States to promote its policies. There are all kinds of diplomatic and economic strategies available to a powerful country like the United States. And, when all else fails, even limited military action is possible, without the hypocrisy involved in acting secretly.

Besides, the critics say, everything the Americans did covertly in Afghanistan could have been done just as well overtly. In fact, the "secret" operation there wasn't really secret at all. The Soviets were aware that Americans were supplying the rebels. It would have been no more dangerous for the United States to have done so openly. And it would have been more honest.

Rather than reducing the risk of war, critics argue, covert military operations increase it. It is a risk that goes up, rather than down, when operations are conducted in secret, without the knowledge and consent of Congress and the people.

As Republican Senator William S. Cohen of Maine has warned, "the president might, indeed, formulate a covert [action] which could bring us to the brink of war with another nation."[5] In fact, some argue that presidents already have. The United States was led into the Vietnam War at least partly by covert activities in Vietnam and Laos. Do we really want to be led to the brink of war without any chance for Congress, or the American public, to consider the matter?

IS COVERT ACTION EFFECTIVE?

Is the "third option" practical? Is covert action an effective tool of foreign policy? Does it work? We have already discussed several examples of covert operations that supporters believe prove that it does. And yet, opponents of covert activities insist that their value is vastly overrated.

Even some ex-officials who have supported covert actions in the past have come to question their actual effectiveness. Ray Cline has admitted that all the "big covert programs of the 1970s came to grief."[6] McGeorge Bundy, one of President Kennedy's national security advisers, goes even farther. He claims that "the dismal historical record of covert military and paramilitary operations over the past twenty-five years is entirely clear."[7] And Admiral Bobby Inman, an ex–deputy director of the CIA under President Ronald Reagan, warns that "the potential value of covert action is greatly overemphasized, and [its potential] problems tend to be neglected."[8]

Critics argue that too many covert actions don't just fail; they make things worse. Even the best of them, some critics charge, provide only short-term solutions to long-term problems. Take some of the successes discussed in this book.

True, they admit, the CIA succeeded in replacing Mossadeq with Shah Reza Pahlavi in 1953. But that "success" planted the seeds of anti-American bitterness that resulted in the humiliating Iranian hostage crisis twenty-six years later.

Jacobo Arbenz Guzmán may have been a bad choice for president of Guatemala in 1954, but he was the elected president of that country. At the time the CIA staged the mock invasion that threw him from power, Guatemala had a working democratic system. It has not had one since. More than

150,000 people have been killed in political violence in Guatemala in the years since the coup. According to a recent report of the human rights group Amnesty International, "suspected critics" of the government are to this day being "subjected to arbitrary seizure, torture, 'disappearance,' and extrajudicial execution."[9] It is, the opponents of covert action point out, hardly a legacy for the CIA to be proud of.

Even the CIA-supported victory of the rebels over the Soviets in Afghanistan was only partial at best, the critics argue. The Soviets are gone, but the Afghan government remains in the hands of Communists. The bloody rebellion drags on and shows no sign of ending.

Supporters agree that many covert actions fail to achieve their goals. But so, they point out, do all other strategies, from diplomatic negotiations to conventional warfare. The fact that a weapon sometimes fails is no reason to get rid of it.

Nor, they argue, is the fact that covert victories are often temporary a reason to abandon covert activities. The CIA-backed Hmong army could not finally defeat the combined forces of the Pathet Lao and the North Vietnamese, but it held them off for ten years. Those were ten years that might not have been possible without covert action.

Even the most disastrous covert operation is not proof that all covert operations should be abandoned, say their supporters. It is true, for example, that the mission to rescue the hostages in Iran failed in the desert. But, that doesn't mean we should forswear the ability to launch covert rescue operations in the future. After all, the Israelis rescued over 100 hostages held by terrorists in Entebbe, Uganda, in 1976. Shouldn't we hold open the chance to do the same? Do we really want to abandon all future hostages forever?

Despite its occasional failures, supporters insist, covert action remains a valuable option—a weapon America needs to keep in its arsenal. "Anybody that does not believe that covert actions can be used effectively in the conduct of foreign policy," says Senator Hatch, "is not living in the real world."[10]

DOES AMERICA HAVE A RIGHT TO INTERFERE IN THE AFFAIRS OF OTHER COUNTRIES?

By definition, covert action involves interfering in the internal affairs of another country. And yet, as Victor Marchetti has written, "The other countries of the world have a fundamental right not to have any outside power interfere in their internal affairs."[11] It is the same right the United States has not to be interfered with by them.

That fundamental right is enshrined in the charter of the United Nations and in other international agreements signed by the United States. And yet, the United States has carried out thousands of covert operations, large and small, around the world.[12] How can this massive interference in the affairs of other countries be justified? Marchetti, along with many other critics of covert action, believes that it can't.

Supporters of covert action claim interference can be justified on the grounds of national security. If the right to be free of interference is recognized in international law, they argue, so is the right to defend oneself. And the right of self-defense, they argue, overrides all other national rights. Other countries sometimes present threats to the national security of the United States, they say. This is particularly true of the Communist countries, and countries, like Iran, that support anti-American terrorists. The United States has a fundamental right to protect itself against those threats, militarily or in any other way—including covert action.

Opponents of covert action complain that this argument is based on a false notion of self-defense. They argue that the right to self-defense only includes defense against direct military or terrorist attack. Very few covert operations are designed to fend off this kind of attack. Most take place far away from the borders of the United States. What is more, they are often directed at countries too small, or too poor, to present any real threat of attack to the United States.

In fact, critics of covert operations point out, many don't involve enemies of the United States at all. The first head of government ever unseated by the CIA was President Quirino of the Philippines. And Quirino, the critics point out, was a close friend and ally of the United States.

"What happened to self-determination of peoples?" asks former senator George McGovern.[13] Critics like McGovern argue that the United States should live up to its own best ideals. One of those ideals, they insist, is the right of people to choose their own governments. When the United States uses covert action to undermine a foreign government, whether friendly or hostile, it is violating that ideal.

IS SECRECY ACCEPTABLE IN A DEMOCRATIC SOCIETY?

For some critics, the main objection to covert action has nothing to do with its effectiveness or with its effect on other nations. It has to do with its effect on the United States. These critics argue that there is something undemocratic—and fundamentally hostile to the American ideal—about the government hiding what it is doing from the people.

Supporters of covert action argue that secrecy is often needed for a variety of good reasons. The most obvious reason is the need to deceive our enemies. The less they know about what we are doing, the less able they will be to defend themselves against it.

Another reason for secrecy is the need to protect our agents and allies. This is a need that U.S. officials have recognized from the beginning. As President James Polk explained a century and a half ago, "In time of . . . impending danger the situation may make it necessary to employ individuals . . . who could never be prevailed on to act if they entertained the least apprehension that their names or their agency would . . . be divulged."[14] This is especially true when those "individuals" are representatives of foreign governments, or when they are acting under cover in dangerous situations.

Most critics would agree that the need to deceive an enemy or to protect an agent may sometimes justify keeping a secret. But the need to fool an enemy, they point out, is usually temporary. Once an operation is over, there is rarely any reason to keep it hidden from the enemy any longer. And the need to protect an agent, they say, is often a smokescreen. Many covert operations could be admitted and explained to the American people without disclosing the identities of the people who took part.

Besides, they argue, those are not the main reasons covert operations are kept secret. Often, they claim, activities are kept secret for no reason other than the love of secrecy itself. This reason (or lack of a reason) is reflected in an argument for secrecy put forward by William Colby in his book *Honorable Men.* Defending the fact that the CIA-backed war in Laos was hidden from the public, Colby explained that "the operation was part of the CIA budget."[15] Since the CIA budget was secret, the

Laotian war had to be kept secret too. This kind of argument is ridiculous, the critics protest. It could be used to justify concealing virtually anything from the American public. Anything the CIA does, Colby seems to be saying, must be kept secret simply because the CIA does it.

Opponents of covert action suspect that the real reason for secrecy has nothing to do with deceiving enemies, protecting agents, or even safeguarding the CIA's budget. Government actions are kept secret primarily to conceal them from the American people. The government is worried either because what it is doing is illegal, or because it would be so unpopular if it became known that the people would demand a stop to it.

What is more, the opponents charge, the government does not stop at refraining from telling what it is doing. All too often, it lies about it. It publicly denies its real activities, sometimes even insisting that it is doing the opposite.

The record of covert action is filled with examples of high government officials lying to the American people. In 1958, for example, there was a revolt against President Sukarno of Indonesia. The U.S. secretary of state, John Foster Dulles, assured Congress that the United States was not involved, and President Eisenhower publicly declared that "our policy is one of careful neutrality." Both were lying; the CIA was backing the coup attempt.[16]

In the 1980s, when word got out that the United States had sold weapons to Iran, President Reagan went on television to speak to the nation. "The charge has been made," he declared, "that the United States has shipped weapons to Iran as payment for the release of American hostages. . . . Those charges are utterly false." But, as investigations later proved, the charges were true.

Whom was President Reagan trying to fool? the

critics ask. Not the Iranians. They knew the United States had sold them the weapons in order to get the hostages released. It was only the American public who didn't know, along with most of the U.S. Congress. And it was only the Americans who were likely to be fooled by the president's denial. President Reagan said what he did because he knew that dealing with Iran was a very unpopular thing to do. It was directly opposed to his publicly stated claim that he would make no deal with the Iranians.

Lying to the people, the opponents of secrecy maintain, does more than deceive them about a particular action or policy. It undermines the system of democracy itself. It runs counter to the democratic values on which our society is based. In a democratic system, the people are supposed to control their government. They pick their leaders. If they are unhappy about what those leaders are doing, they throw them out and pick others to take their place. But how can the people control their government if they don't know what it is doing? How can they judge the nation's leaders if they don't know where they are leading?

Secrecy undermines democracy in another way as well, say the critics. It breaks the bond of trust between the people and their leaders. It undermines the faith the people have in the honesty and honor of their own government.

Most supporters of covert action would probably agree that secrecy should not be used merely to avoid domestic political problems. But, they would argue, there is often a broader foreign policy purpose behind what seems to be a narrow political motive. The president, they argue, is often in a better position to judge what should be done than the public at large. The president is elected to protect the United States from its enemies. It is the president's duty to do whatever needs to be done to protect America's interests, whether the public or the Congress understands that need or not. The ex-senator and presidential adviser John Tower put it this way: "The people's right to protection outweighs their right to know."[17]

If that is so, the critics of secrecy respond, the president should say so. The president should openly do what the president believes needs to be done, and then take the political consequences, whatever they may be.

IS COVERT ACTION IMMORAL?

Richard Helms has a simple explanation for the hostility many people feel toward covert action. They dislike it, he says, because "they think it's nasty."[18]

Helms, an ex-director of the CIA, clearly believes that people who think that way are naive. His use of the word *nasty* is meant sarcastically. But there is no question that covert operations often require people to take part in some unpleasant activities, activities that most people would ordinarily consider both "nasty" and immoral.

In 1954, a government commission declared that in the covert war against international Communism "There are no rules." What is more, it said, the traditionally "acceptable norms of human conduct do not apply."[19] This moral standard, or lack of a standard, seems to have been applied by many of the people who conduct covert actions. Covert agents have often been accused of activities outside the "acceptable norms of human conduct." These include cooperating with "death squads" in Latin American countries, and helping to train and supply police torturers in Iran and elsewhere.

Perhaps the most morally controversial of all covert activities is political assassination. Officially, the CIA has never admitted carrying out assassinations. Nonetheless, there is clear evidence that the CIA has been involved in planning, if not in actually carrying out, assassinations of several foreign leaders. What is more, CIA agents have clearly encouraged others to carry out political murders of lower-level foreign officials and civilians in several countries.

In the 1970s, a Senate investigating committee uncovered past CIA plans to assassinate Cuba's Fidel Castro and Patrice Lumumba of the Congo (now Zaire) among others.[20] It was in these plots that the CIA came closest to the kinds of exploits that are described in adventure novels and movies. At least one of the plots against Castro was invented by E. Howard Hunt, who also wrote spy novels in his spare time.[21]

There were at least eight different attempts to assassinate Castro in the first five years of the 1960s.[22] One of them made use of the fact that Castro was a heavy smoker of Cuba's famous Havana cigars. It involved lacing his cigars with a deadly poison. Another plan called for him to be killed with a poisoned pen. At one point, the CIA even made a deal with the head of a Mafia crime family, Sam Giancana, to murder Castro for the Agency.

As far as the public knows, the attempts on Castro were made without direct orders from any president. Nonetheless, when it attacked Castro, the CIA clearly believed it was carrying out the wishes of President John Kennedy. As Richard Helms, then director of the CIA, later explained to a Senate committee: "It was made abundantly clear . . . that the desire was to get rid of the Castro regime and to get rid of Castro." Although the president did not specifically order the CIA to kill Castro, Helms testified, he put "no limits . . . on this injunction."[23]

The plots against Castro obviously failed. He still

rules Cuba today. Whether any CIA attempts to kill foreign heads of government ever succeeded is not known. Most defenders of the CIA, including William Colby, say no.[24] But according to several ex–CIA agents, including John Stockwell, who served in Angola, the CIA has been involved in supporting people who did succeed in assassinating foreign leaders.[25] What is more, at least a few of those leaders the CIA made plans to kill (including Lumumba and the Dominican Republic dictator Rafael Trujillo) were assassinated, whether or not the CIA played a direct role in their deaths.

Following the Senate committee's revelations, President Gerald Ford acted to deflect criticism. In February 1976, he issued an executive order to end all U.S. involvement in efforts to assassinate foreign leaders.

There is, however, evidence that the CIA continued to encourage foreign assassination attempts despite the ban. In 1983, it was revealed that the CIA had distributed a handbook called *Psychological Operations in Guerilla Warfare* to Contra guerrillas fighting the leftist Sandinista government in Nicaragua. The handbook suggested that the Contras carry out "selective" assassinations of low-level Sandinistas in the countryside.[26]

There have been many other charges that CIA agents and officials have been involved in assassination attempts as well. In his book *Veil*, reporter Bob Woodward charged that CIA director William Casey helped launch one of the bloodiest of them. According to Woodward, Casey personally arranged with the Saudi Arabian ambassador to the United States to have a terrorist leader named Sheikh Fadlallah killed in Beirut, Lebanon. The attempt was made by exploding a car bomb near Fadlallah's home on March 8, 1985. Eighty bystanders were killed, and 200 others were wounded, but Fadlallah escaped.[27]

The "nastiness" of covert operations includes much more than the direct violence involved in activities like guerrilla warfare and assassination. Lies, betrayal, and corruption are common elements of almost all covert activities. A parade of ex–CIA agents have described working hand in hand with terrorists, murderers, drug smugglers, and traitors. They have sometimes had to recruit these people, and even pay them for their services. (Even Manuel Noriega, the drug-running criminal and until recently the dictator of Panama, was once on the CIA payroll.)

Caleb Bach, who recruited foreign agents for the CIA in South America and Mexico, has described the effects these activities have on the people who conduct them. He says that the profession "contaminates" the personal lives of CIA agents. It "destroys those elements of personal decency that we value in our lives."[28] Carl Eiffler, who led the bloody but effective OSS operation in Burma, went even further. Decades later, he acknowledged that he had broken "every law of God and man." Someday, he feared, he would have to pay for it. "Not to man, to God."[29]

Defenders of covert action argue that, however unfortunate it may be, the "nastiness" involved in covert activities is one price that has to be paid for national security. But, ultimately, the question must be asked: Should the United States pay this kind of moral price? Should its agents—acting in the name of the American people—take part in activities that destroy their sense of personal decency and break "every law of God and man"? Opponents argue that this price is far too high, particularly considering the questionable benefits the country receives from its covert operations.

8

OVERSIGHT—THE STRUGGLE FOR CONTROL OF COVERT ACTION

Whether for good or bad, covert action has been a weapon of American foreign policy throughout our history. Even with all the controversy that surrounds it, covert action is not likely to be abandoned anytime soon.

Even many of the critics who demand an end to all covert paramilitary operations stop short of calling for the end of covert action altogether. There are few who would go as far as Victor Marchetti, who argues that "[t]he time has come for the United States to stand openly behind its actions overseas, to lead by example rather than manipulation."[1] Most believe that there are some circumstances, however rare, in which covert activities of some kind would be useful and justified.

Because of this, the major concerns of both supporters and critics of "the third option" center around how it should be used. How can this dangerous weapon be controlled to make sure that it helps to protect America's peace and security instead of endangering them?

It is clear that the details of specific covert actions cannot be publicly debated in advance. Therefore, the question of *how* to direct and control covert activities boils down to the question of *who* should control them. Who should decide when and how they should be used?

CHECKS AND BALANCES

"Covert actions," as Harry Rositzke has pointed out, "are mounted to avoid official responsibility."[2] And yet, someone *has* to be responsible for covert activities. Whatever the public is told, someone in the government must have the final power to say, "Yes, this should be done," or "No, this must not be done." Traditionally, that person has been the president of the United States.

Some presidents have exercised their control directly. George Washington personally sent agents abroad to influence foreign leaders. James Madison personally sent George Mathews into Florida, without even telling his secretary of state. Other presidents have turned over most of the management of covert activities to someone else. Most recent presidents, for example, have relied primarily on the CIA.

But covert action has been recognized as a function of the executive branch of government from the beginning. Ultimately, it has been the responsibility of the president. Most of the political controversy over how covert action ought to be directed and controlled has centered on the extent to which Congress ought to be involved as well.

As every schoolchild knows, the American system of government is built on checks and balances. The executive is only one of three branches of government, the others being the legislative and judicial branches. In most matters, each branch acts as a check and balance to the others. Congress makes the laws, which the judicial and executive branches carry out, but the president has the power to veto laws he or she objects to. The president has the power to appoint judges to the courts, but only with the "advice and consent" of the Senate. And the courts have the power to declare actions of both the executive and legislative branches unconstitutional, etc.

But when it comes to covert action, this system of checks and balances breaks down: most presidents have exercised their power to order covert activities in almost complete independence from the other branches of government.

At best, presidents have set up internal checks within the executive branch itself. Some have set up one or more committees to pass judgment on, and to oversee, covert activities. President Eisenhower, for example, had two: the President's Board of Consultants on Foreign Intelligence Activities, and the so-called 5412 Group.[3] President Reagan set up the President's Intelligence Oversight Board in 1981 to warn him of any intelligence activities that might violate a law or presidential order.[4] But such executive agencies were answerable only to the president himself. They provided no real check on the president's power to conduct covert activities, either abroad or at home.

It was an abuse of presidential power that took place right here in the United States that prompted the first real push for congressional oversight in the 1970s.

WATERGATE

Early in the morning of June 17, 1972, five men were arrested breaking into the headquarters of the Democratic National Committee in the Watergate building in Washington, D.C. The police soon arrested others who had been involved in the break-in as well.

At first, the incident was regarded as an ordi-

111

nary burglary. This began to change when police discovered that some of the men had ties to the government. Some had worked for the CIA. At least one worked directly for the White House. Suspicion began to grow that the break-in had something to do with President Richard Nixon's campaign for reelection.

As it turned out, the suspicion was right. The burglars were part of a secret organization known as the Plumbers. It got its name from the fact that it had been formed to stop "leaks" of government information to the press. But its original purpose had been lost in a maze of other activities, most of which were designed to make sure that President Nixon was reelected in 1972.

The Plumbers group was only one of several covert groups working out of either the White House or Nixon's reelection committee.[5] The president turned to them instead of to the CIA because the Agency was forbidden to conduct covert actions inside the United States—much less involve itself in domestic politics.

But the men in charge of the Plumbers were veterans of the CIA. They had extensive backgrounds in covert activities. One of them, E. Howard Hunt, had been a key figure in both the Bay of Pigs operation and in Operation Mongoose. Both put their experience to use in their new job.

The Plumbers and the other secret groups were essentially covert action agencies. They were different from the older, more traditional agencies in several ways. For one thing, they operated less as arms of the United States government than as arms of the president. For another, their activities were concentrated in the United States. And, most significantly of all, their actions were directed more toward promoting domestic political goals than toward furthering American foreign policy.

The "president's men," as a popular book would

112

call them, carried out a wide variety of illegal activities. They "bugged" (or tapped) the phones of reporters and government officials alike. They sabotaged the campaigns of Democratic candidates. They even broke into a psychiatrist's office in order to steal the medical files of a patient. And finally, of course, they burglarized the Democratic headquarters in the Watergate office building.

The Plumbers, and the others in the White House who worked with them, justified their illegal activities on the grounds that they were carrying out the wishes of the president. They believed the president had the right to authorize activities that would otherwise be illegal in order to protect the national security. What is more, they were convinced that the president's reelection was vital to that security. They considered Senator George McGovern, the Democratic nominee for president, to be a dangerous leftist.

In the wake of the failed burglary, the president directed a wide-ranging effort to cover up his own involvement with the Plumbers' activities. Among other steps in the cover-up, money was paid to the arrested burglars to make sure that they would not reveal their relationship to his campaign. It was a desperate effort to keep plausible deniability.

One part of the cover-up involved the CIA. People working for the White House approached the Agency to ask for help. On one occasion, they asked the CIA to conceal evidence. On another, they asked the Agency to provide secret bail money for the burglars. The Agency turned down both requests.[6]

When the CIA refused to cooperate willingly, the White House tried to take advantage of the CIA's policy of silence about covert activities to make the Agency a scapegoat. It spread rumors that the whole thing had been a CIA operation, in which the White House had not been involved. This was made easier by the fact that the FBI, which was investigating the break-in, suspected that the CIA might be behind it.[7]

Many people wondered, in the words of Senator Frank Church, if the CIA had become a "rogue elephant." Was it out of control, conducting covert operations not only abroad but in the United States as well, without consulting the president or anyone else? Years later, some of the "president's men" would continue to insist that the CIA had been behind Watergate.[8]

In his book *The CIA and the Cult of Intelligence*, Victor Marchetti claimed that the CIA had in fact given some technical assistance to the Plumbers.[9] But, if so, it seems clear that the CIA was doing a favor for the White House, not acting as "rogue elephant." As a 1976 report of the House Select Committee on Intelligence concluded: "All evidence . . . suggests that the CIA, far from being out of control, has been utterly responsive to the instructions of the President. . . ."[10]

In any case, most Americans at first believed President Nixon when he denied any connection to the Watergate affair. They couldn't believe that the president of the United States was involved in what was laughingly called a "third-rate burglary." In the election that November, President Nixon was swept back into office in one of the biggest landslides in American history. But, thanks largely to the efforts of two reporters for the *Washington Post*, the facts eventually came to light.[11] The true extent of the covert activities, and the president's involvement in them, was finally revealed—but not until months after the election.

The press reports prompted a congressional investigation of the whole Watergate affair. When a House committee recommended that President Nixon be impeached (charged with criminal offenses), he resigned in disgrace. He was the first president ever to do so.

The discovery that the president had used his power to conduct covert activities against his political opponents outraged many Americans. It raised the question of what other outrageous things presidents had done—or might do in the future—under the cloak of secrecy.

Committees in both houses of Congress launched investigations of the activities of the intelligence agencies. The House committee was chaired by Representative Otis Pike of New York, and the Senate committee by Senator Frank Church of Idaho. Together, they made the most sweeping congressional investigation into the world of covert activities in history. The Church committee alone gathered more than 8,000 pages of testimony in hundreds of sessions, conducted more than 800 interviews outside the hearings themselves, and received fourteen official briefings from the CIA.[12] Spurred on by the committees' efforts, the press began many investigations of its own.

What all these investigations uncovered deeply shocked many Americans. They were particularly disturbed to discover the extent of the administration's efforts to destroy its political opposition. One of the most appalled was Walter Mondale, a member of the Church committee who would be the Democratic nominee for president in 1984. Senator Mondale described the covert attacks on the Democrats as "the tip of an iceberg that could have destroyed American liberty."[13]

OVERSIGHT MEASURES

The Watergate scandal brought new demands for changes in the way covert activities were conducted. Some members of Congress became convinced that the president—*any* president—could no longer be trusted to act in total secrecy. They called for Congress to oversee the covert activities of the executive branch. It was, they argued, the best way to extend the principle of checks and balances, as it applied to the rest of the federal government, to the world of covert activities.

Congressional oversight made sense, they argued, because Congress provided the funds that made covert action possible. It had done so ever since the very first Congress voted George Washington his secret fund in 1790. It was only fair, then, that Congress should have a way to find out whether the money was being well spent.

The first step toward congressional oversight came with the Hughes-Ryan Amendment in December 1974. It ordered that no congressionally authorized funds be spent on any covert operation unless certain conditions were met. First, the president had to make a "finding" that the operation was "important" to the country's security. Then, the president had to inform several important congressional committees about the operation "in a timely fashion."[14] Just what "a timely fashion" meant wasn't defined. This loophole allowed the president to keep a "finding" secret long after the authorized operation had begun.

The Congressional Oversight Act of 1980 reformed the Hughes-Ryan reporting requirements. For one thing, it reduced the number of committees that had to be told about covert activities from eight to two: the intelligence committees of the Senate and the House. But it required that those committees be kept "fully and currently informed of all intelligence activities."

This meant, among other things, that they had to be told about covert operations *before* they took place, if at all possible. If "extraordinary circumstances" made notifying the committees in advance impossible, the president had to notify key congressional leaders instead. There were eight of those leaders, four from each major party. They were the Speaker and the minority leader of the House, the majority and minority leaders of the Senate, and the chairperson and ranking minority party members of both the House and the Senate intelligence committees.

Like the Hughes-Ryan Amendment, the 1980 Oversight Act required only that the committees be informed. It didn't give them the right to veto proposed covert actions. It did, however, allow committee members to comment on them, and even to tell other congressional committees about them if they thought it necessary.

AVOIDING OVERSIGHT IN NICARAGUA AND IRAN

The people who plan and carry out covert actions have always resented congressional oversight, considering it an unjustified interference in the affairs of the executive branch.

Both the Ford and Carter administrations interpreted the oversight laws more loosely than Congress did. This was particularly true when it came to the phrase "timely fashion." Many members of Congress assumed that "timely fashion" required prior notice of covert actions. Administration officials argued that it required that Congress be informed within a reasonable time *after* an operation was under way. President Carter, for example, did not notify Congress in advance of the Delta commando mission to rescue the hostages in Iran.[15]

But the Ford and Carter administrations at least tried to follow the spirit, if not the letter, of the oversight laws. The Reagan administration, on the other hand, did its best to avoid both. President Reagan and his CIA director, William Casey, used covert action more than either Ford or Carter had done. They were so fond of secrecy, in fact, that Senator Patrick Leahy accused them of having an "obsession with covert actions."[16]

This "obsession" was particularly noticeable when it came to dealing with the leftist Sandinista government of Nicaragua. Both the president and the CIA director were determined to destroy the Sandinistas, and again and again they turned to covert action to do it. Their efforts were similar to Operation Mongoose in the 1960s.

Like the earlier attack on Fidel Castro, the new covert war was designed to destroy a country's government by destroying its economy. Also like the attack on Castro, the new war was fought on several fronts. One of them, known as Operation Yellowfruit, was conducted by an Army Special Operations unit. Using Defense Department funds, it participated in various covert military activities against Nicaragua, including attacks on Nicaraguan airfields.[17] Another involved recruiting and training a paramilitary force, called the Contras, made up of Nicaraguan exiles.

CIA director Casey, in particular, had a low opinion of the House and Senate Intelligence Committees. Also, he knew that key members of Congress, including the Speaker of the House of Representatives, Tip O'Neill, were bitterly opposed to the administration's policy in Nicaragua. For both these reasons, he was reluctant to inform Congress about what the administration was doing there.

In 1982, O'Neill and another House member, Edward P. Boland, pushed an amendment through Congress that was designed to do just what Casey had feared—prevent the administration from carrying out its Nicaraguan policy. It forbade the government to give money to anyone, including the Contras, "for the purpose of overthrowing the government of Nicaragua."[18] The so-called Boland Amendment didn't dampen Casey's and Reagan's enthusiasm for the covert war. It only made them even more reluctant to tell Congress about it.

In 1984, the CIA laid mines in the waters of Nicaragua's harbors. The idea was to disrupt the Nicaraguan economy by discouraging foreign ships from delivering oil and other vital imports.[19] In order for the plan to work, the fact that the mines were there had to be more or less public knowledge. Even so, the administration did not inform Congress it had mined the harbors until after the Nicaraguan government complained and the operation had been exposed in both the Nicaraguan and American press.[20]

Angered by the mining, and most of all by the fact that it had not been informed, Congress stopped all aid to the Contras. What is more, it forbade any further help to the Contras by government officials.[21] Casey apologized. Negotiations were held that came up with new guidelines for reporting covert activities to Congress. The administration agreed to inform Congress in the future of all presidential findings that approved covert actions *before* those actions began, except in the most "extraordinary" circumstances.

Despite the agreement, Congress had to learn of the next major covert operation involving Nicaragua the way it had learned about the last one—in the press.

PRIVATIZING COVERT ACTION— THE "ENTERPRISE"

Following the mining of Nicaraguan harbors, the Reagan administration's CIA chief William Casey set out to avoid congressional oversight by using a private, nongovernment organization to act in the CIA's place. It was organized by two businessmen, retired Air Force Major General Richard Secord and

119

Albert Hakim, and a Marine lieutenant colonel named Oliver North who worked for the White House. The new organization was so secret that it didn't even have a name. Among themselves, its participants simply referred to it as the "Enterprise." It presents a good example of the special dangers involved when covert action is entrusted to an agency entirely outside the checks and balances of government—especially an agency whose own existence is a secret.

North, who was a skillful fund-raiser, used his White House connection to raise money from wealthy Americans who wanted to help the Contras. Meanwhile, North, Secord, and Hakim negotiated a major sale of American weapons to Iran. Some of the profits from the sale were then secretly sent to the Contras in Nicaragua.

Neither the United States nor the Iranian government wanted it known that they were dealing with each other. Both governments knew that the arrangement would be extremely unpopular among their own peoples. Most Iranians still blamed the United States for putting the hated Shah in power, while most Americans still considered Iran an outlaw nation. They blamed it for supporting the terrorists who were holding several Americans hostage in Lebanon.

The "Enterprise" was designed to achieve a number of purposes all at once. First, its arms deal was intended to get the American hostages in Lebanon released. Second, by not using money directly authorized by Congress, it would enable the administration to bypass the Boland Amendment and still give weapons to the Contras. And third, it would provide a way to avoid reporting any of the covert dealings to Congress at all. The attempt to avoid the reporting requirement was obviously important to the administration. The "finding" the president signed authorizing the arms sale to Iran

120

*Depending on your politics,
Oliver North, the leading
figure in the Iran-Contra
scandal, is a villain, a hero,
a martyr, or the fall guy.*

actually contained an order forbidding the CIA to tell Congress about it.[22]

But the "Enterprise" had another, much larger purpose as well. According to testimony given by Oliver North before a congressional committee investigating the affair, Casey hoped it would become a new kind of *super*-secret covert action agency. In North's words, it would be an "existing, off-the-shelf, self-sustaining, stand-alone entity, independent of appropriated moneys." In other words, it would not depend on Congress for its funds, even indirectly. Congress wouldn't even know about it.

The "Enterprise" continued in secrecy until late 1986, when a newsmagazine in Beirut, Lebanon, reported that a high U.S. official had negotiated a secret weapons deal with the government of Iran.[23]

Most Americans found it hard to believe that the United States had dealt with Iran at all, much less sold weapons to it. Iran had humiliated the United States during the hostage crisis of 1979, and it was still supporting the forces who held hostages in Lebanon. President Reagan had insisted that he would never make any kind of a deal for the hostages' release. But over the next few months, details of the so-called Iran-Contra affair came to light. Congressional hearings were held, and ultimately, several people, including Oliver North, were charged with crimes growing out of the affair. Their crimes included lying to Congress about the government's covert activities.

RELAXING THE RULES

In the wake of the Iran-Contra scandal, there were loud demands for new laws to make sure that such things would never happen again. Bills were introduced in Congress to strengthen oversight. In the meantime, William Casey died, and a new director was appointed who seemed more willing to cooperate with Congress. For a time, the pendulum seemed to be swinging away from the covert agencies and toward more congressional oversight.

As it turned out, however, the pendulum didn't swing far. George Bush, the president who followed Ronald Reagan, had once served as director of the CIA himself. Soon after Bush's election, the Speaker of the House of Representatives, Jim Wright, announced that Congress would drop the effort to strengthen congressional oversight as a "gesture of good faith" to the new president.[24]

It wasn't long before the pendulum began to swing back the other way. The swing began with a failed coup attempt by Panamanian Army officers in Panama. For years, the United States had been trying to find a way to remove Manuel Noriega, the Panamanian "strongman," from power. Noriega, who had once been employed by the CIA while he was head of Panama's security forces, was an international criminal. A federal court in Florida had indicted him for helping to smuggle cocaine from South America to the United States.

But there was little the United States could do to bring Noriega to trial. The U.S. government could not get the Panamanian courts to send him to the United States because Noriega controlled the government of Panama. When a political opponent was elected president in a Panamanian election, Noriega simply overruled the voters. He even had the winner beaten up by thugs in the street, just to emphasize the completeness of his power.

Then, in 1989, rebel military forces in Panama staged a coup to unseat Noriega. Although the details of what happened are not clear, the coup failed and the rebel leaders were killed. The Bush administration came under heavy criticism in the United States for not sending American military forces stationed in Panama to help the rebels.

The administration defended itself by complaining that its hands had been tied. It argued that it could not help the rebels because of the rules forbidding U.S. involvement in assassinations abroad. As it interpreted those rules, the U.S. government could not support a coup if there were any chance at all that it might result in the death of a foreign leader.

What is more, the administration claimed, under some interpretations of the rules, the CIA might even be required to *warn* a foreign dictator that there might be an attack on his or her life.

Under public pressure from the Bush administration, the Senate committee in charge of oversight drew up new rules. They gave Bush and future presidents greater freedom to cooperate with foreign coup attempts.

But they went farther. They also relaxed the requirements for notifying Congress of covert operations. Instead of demanding to be told of covert activities within forty-eight hours, as they had insisted before, the committee now agreed to remove any specific deadline. They accepted the president's promise that he would tell them about planned actions beforehand if he could, and within a reasonable number of days afterward if that wasn't possible.

To opponents of covert action, this new faith in a president's word seemed astonishing. Only the year before, one senator had complained on the Senate floor of "a pattern of abuse, improper behavior, contempt for congressional oversight, and outright lying that goes back to the early 1980s."[25]

But some supporters of covert action, like ex–CIA director Richard Helms, complained that even these looser restrictions were too tight.[26] Despite such complaints, the new rules were widely taken to signal a move toward freer use of covert action by the CIA and other government agencies.

LOOKING TO THE FUTURE

The pendulum may swing back in the direction of greater congressional oversight sometime in the future. New, stronger laws may still be passed. But the evidence suggests that the laws that are passed may not matter very much in the long run.

After all, congressional oversight did not stop the Carter administration from launching the hostage rescue without notifying Congress. Congressional demands that aid to the Contras be ended did not stop the Reagan administration from forming the "Enterprise" and supplying the Contras anyway. Not even a presidential ban on assassinations stopped the director of the CIA from helping to plan the botched assassination of Sheikh Fadlallah.

As Senator Patrick Leahy remarked in the Senate debate over an oversight bill in 1988: "Laws can only be as effective as the willingness of people to obey them. All the reform bills in the world will do nothing if those in the administration and the intelligence agencies who propose, carry out, and oversee covert actions do not change how they think."[27]

Just how their thinking needs to change was suggested many years ago by the renowned journalist Walter Lippmann. Soon after the Bay of Pigs invasion in 1961, he concluded that "The United States, like every other government, must employ secret agents. But the United States cannot successfully conduct large secret conspiracies. . . . The American conscience is a reality. It will make hesitant and ineffectual, even if it does not prevent, an un-American policy. It follows that . . . we must find our strength by developing and applying our own principles, not in abandoning them."[28]

Again in the words of Senator Leahy: "One last thing: We can write every law possible; we can anticipate every contingency conceivable. But unless the people to whom these laws apply are willing to follow them, they go for naught."[29]

SOURCE NOTES

CHAPTER ONE

1. National Security Council Directive 10/2, quoted in John Prados, *Presidents' Secret Wars: CIA and Pentagon Covert Operations Since World War II* (New York: William Morrow, 1986), p. 29.
2. U.S. Senate, *Final Report of the Select Committee to Study Governmental Operations with Respect to Intelligence Activities*, 94th Congress, 2nd Session (Washington, D.C.: U.S. Government Printing Office), p. 620.
3. Prados, p. 29.
4. *Final Report . . .* p. 620.

CHAPTER TWO

1. Richard N. Current, T. Harry William, and Frank Freidel, *American History: A Survey*, 4th ed. (New York: Knopf, 1975), p. 809.
2. Bob Woodward, *Veil: The Secret Wars of the CIA, 1981–87* (New York: Pocket Books, 1987).
3. *Intelligence in the War of Independence* (Washington, D.C.: CIA, 1976).

4. Rhodri Jeffreys-Jones, *American Espionage: From Secret Service to CIA* (New York: The Free Press, 1977), p. 11.
5. William R. Corson, *The Armies of Ignorance* (New York: Dial Press/James Wade, 1977), p. 520.
6. The Mathews expedition is described in ibid., pp. 515–516.
7. Ibid., p. 520.
8. Ibid., p. 536.
9. Jeffreys-Jones, p. 34.
10. Ibid., p. 24.
11. Corson, pp. 593–594.
12. Jeffreys-Jones, p. 27.
13. Corson, p. 599.
14. Jeffreys-Jones, p. 42.

CHAPTER THREE

1. William Stevenson, *A Man Called Intrepid* (New York: Ballantine, 1976), p. 20.
2. For a life of William Donovan, see Cory Ford, *Donovan of OSS* (Boston: Little, Brown, 1970).
3. William R. Corson, *The Armies of Ignorance* (New York: Dial Press/James Wade, 1977), p. 113.
4. Ray S. Cline, *Secrets, Spies and Scholars: Blueprint of the Essential CIA* (Washington, D.C.: Acropolis, 1976), p. 33.
5. Phillip Knightley, *The Second Oldest Profession: Spies and Spying in the Twentieth Century* (New York: Norton, 1986), p. 222.
6. For more information on the SOE, see M.R.D. Foot, "Was SOE Any Good?," and Mark Wheeler, "The SOE Phenomenon," both in Walter Laqueur, ed., *The Second World War* (London: Sage, 1982).
7. Corson, p. 179.
8. Cline, p. 49.

9. Ibid., p. 51.

10. Knightley, p. 225.

11. Corson, p. 176.

12. CIA director William Casey, in a speech given to a meeting of ex–OSS members in 1986, in an excerpt shown on the three-part television documentary *Secret Intelligence* (copyright 1988 by Community Television of Southern California), which was shown over public television on various dates.

13. Rhodri Jeffreys-Jones, *American Espionage: From Secret Service to CIA* (New York: The Free Press, 1977), pp. 167–168.

14. *Secret Intelligence.*

15. Knightley, p. 221.

16. Cline, pp. 69–70.

17. Gregory F. Treverton, *Covert Action: The Limits of Intervention in the Postwar World* (New York: Basic Books, 1987), p. 32.

18. For an account of NORSO's activities, see William Colby and Peter Forbath, *Honorable Men: My Life in the CIA* (New York: Simon and Schuster, 1978), pp. 44–50.

19. Cline, p. 73.

20. *Secret Intelligence.*

21. John Prados, *Presidents' Secret Wars: CIA and Pentagon Covert Operations Since World War II* (New York: William Morrow, 1986), p. 16.

22. Knightley, p. 237.

23. Prados, pp. 16–17.

24. Knightley, p. 239.

CHAPTER FOUR

1. Ray S. Cline, *Secrets, Spies and Scholars: Blueprint of the Essential CIA* (Washington, D.C.: Acropolis Books, 1976), pp. 19–20.

2. Phillip Knightley, *The Second Oldest Profession: Spies and Spying in the Twentieth Century* (New York: Norton, 1986), p. 222.

3. Rhodri Jeffreys-Jones, *American Espionage: From Secret Service to CIA* (New York: The Free Press, 1977), p. 167.

4. William R. Corson, *The Armies of Ignorance* (New York: Dial Press/James Wade, 1977), pp. 215–216.

5. Tom Braden, "The Birth of the CIA," *American Heritage*, February 1977, p. 6.

6. Quoted by William Colby in Colby and Peter Forbath, *Honorable Men: My Life in the CIA* (New York: Simon and Schuster, 1978), p. 59.

7. Ibid., p. 7.

8. The directive establishing the National Intelligence Authority and the Central Intelligence Group is reprinted in Corson, pp. 274–275.

9. Ibid., p. 276.

10. Colby and Forbath, p. 71.

11. Corson, p. 289.

12. Victor Marchetti and John D. Marks, *The CIA and the Cult of Intelligence* (New York: Knopf, 1974), p. 22.

13. National Security Council Document NSC 1/3, as quoted by Cline, p. 101.

14. Braden, p. 5.

15. John Prados, *Presidents' Secret Wars: CIA and Pentagon Covert Operations Since World War II* (New York: William Morrow, 1986), p. 28.

16. Ibid., p. 29.

17. Eisenhower's farewell address as president, quoted in Richard N. Current, T. Harry William, and Frank Freidel, *American History: A Survey*, 4th ed. (New York: Knopf, 1975), p. 807.

18. Marchetti and Marks, pp. 58–61.

19. Philip Agee, *Inside the Company: CIA Diary* (New York: Stonehill, 1975), p. 8.

20. Gregory F. Treverton, *Covert Action: The Limits of Intervention in the Postwar World* (New York: Basic Books, 1987), p. 40.

21. Bob Woodward, *Veil: The Secret Wars of the CIA, 1981–87* (New York: Pocket Books, 1987), p. 51.

22. Treverton, p. 42.

23. Woodward, p. 358.

CHAPTER FIVE

1. For a brief description of how the U.S. got control of the Philippines, see Michael Kronenwetter, *The Military Power of the President* (New York: Franklin Watts, 1988), pp. 76–77.

2. Russell Johnson, "U.S. Intervention in Cambodia and the Philippines," in *Uncloaking the CIA* (New York: Free Press, 1978), p. 88.

3. H. Bradford Westerfield, *The Instruments of American Foreign Policy* (New York: Crowell, 1963), p. 409.

4. Victor Marchetti and John D. Marks, *The CIA and the Cult of Intelligence* (New York: Knopf, 1974), p. 28.

5. William Colby and Peter Forbath, *Honorable Men: My Life in the CIA* (New York: Simon and Schuster, 1978), p. 104.

6. Westerfield, pp. 414–416.

7. Ibid., p. 415.

8. *Department of State Bulletin*, October 19, 1953, p. 524.

9. Westerfield, p. 418.

10. Interviewed on *Secret Intelligence*, a three-part television documentary (copyright 1988 by Community Television of Southern California) broadcast by public television on various dates.

11. John Prados, *Presidents' Secret Wars: CIA and Pentagon Covert Operations Since World War II* (New York: William Morrow, 1986), p. 92.
12. Gregory F. Treverton, *Covert Action: The Limits of Intervention in the Postwar World* (New York: Basic Books, 1987), p. 56.
13. Prados, p. 95.
14. Interviewed on *Secret Intelligence.*
15. Harry Rositzke, *The CIA's Secret Operations* (New York: Reader's Digest Press, 1977), p. 188.
16. Prados, p. 97.
17. Treverton, p. 55.
18. Prados, p. 98.
19. Treverton, p. 53.
20. For a detailed account of Operation Success, see Richard H. Immerman, *The CIA in Guatemala: The Foreign Policy of Intervention* (Austin: University of Texas Press, 1982).
21. Prados, p. 98.
22. Rositzke, p. 175.
23. Interviewed on *Secret Intelligence.*
24. Ibid.
25. Prados, p. 101.
26. Rositzke, p. 175.
27. Treverton, p. 54.
28. Colby and Forbath, p. 183.
29. NSC Directive 5412/2, quoted in Prados, pp. 112–113.
30. Bob Woodward, *Veil: The Secret Wars of the CIA, 1981–87* (New York: Pocket Books, 1987), p. 68.
31. Treverton, p. 213.
32. Woodward, p. 425.
33. "Legacy of an Unpopular War," *Time,* April 10, 1989, p. 64.
34. Ibid.

CHAPTER SIX

1. For a detailed account of the Bay of Pigs operation, see Peter Wyden, *The Bay of Pigs: The Untold Story* (New York: Simon and Schuster, 1979).
2. Ibid., pp. 87–89.
3. Thomas Powers, *The Man Who Kept the Secrets: Richard Helms and the CIA* (New York: Knopf, 1979), p. 111.
4. Gregory F. Treverton, *Covert Action: The Limits of Intervention in the Postwar World* (New York: Basic Books, 1987), pp. 86–87.
5. Ibid., p. 96.
6. Powers, p. 115.
7. Ibid., p. 114.
8. Treverton, p. 98.
9. From *Secret Intelligence*, a three-part television documentary (copyright 1988 by Community Television of Southern California) broadcast on public television on various dates.
10. Allan Nevins and Henry Steele Commager, *A Pocket History of the United States* (New York: Washington Square Press, 1981), p. 560.
11. Richard N. Current, T. Harry William, and Frank Freidel, *American History: A Survey*, 4th ed. (New York: Knopf, 1975), p. 89.
12. William Colby and Peter Forbath, *Honorable Men: My Life in the CIA* (New York: Simon and Schuster, 1978), p. 184.
13. William R. Corson, *The Armies of Ignorance* (New York: Dial Press/James Wade, 1977), p. 393.
14. For more on the secret war, see John Prados, *Presidents' Secret Wars: CIA and Pentagon Covert Operations Since World War II* (New York: William Morrow, 1986), pp. 210–217.
15. Corson, p. 393.

16. *Secret Intelligence.*
17. Ibid.
18. Jonathan Kwitny, *The Crimes of Patriots* (New York: Simon and Schuster, 1987), p. 22. William Colby defends the operation in Colby and Forbath.
19. Victor Marchetti and John D. Marks, *The CIA and the Cult of Intelligence* (New York: Knopf, 1974), p. 31.
20. Colby and Forbath, p. 192.
21. Harry Rositzke, *The CIA's Secret Operations* (New York: Reader's Digest Press, 1977), p. 181.
22. Prados, p. 271.
23. Ray S. Cline, *Secrets, Spies and Scholars: Blueprint of the Essential CIA* (Washington, D.C.: Acropolis, 1976), p. 215.
24. Colby and Forbath, p. 194.
25. Marchetti and Marks, p. 32.
26. Prados, p. 282.
27. Colby and Forbath, p. 195.
28. Rositzke, p. 181.
29. Colby and Forbath, p. 195.
30. Leon Friedman and Bert Neuborne, *Unquestioning Obedience to the President* (New York: Norton, 1972), quoted in the Introduction by Senator George McGovern, p. 16.
31. Spencer Sherman, "The Hmong in America," *National Geographic*, October 1988, pp. 587–610.
32. That show became today's *Nightline*, seen nightly on ABC-TV.

CHAPTER SEVEN

1. Speech to the Senate, March 4, 1988, published in *Congressional Digest*, December 1988, pp. 301–309.

2. John Prados, *Presidents' Secret Wars: CIA and Pentagon Covert Operations Since World War II* (New York: William Morrow, 1986), p. 403.

3. Ibid., p. 277.

4. Ibid., p. 403.

5. Speech to the Senate, March 3, 1988, published in *Congressional Digest,* December 1988, pp. 308–312.

6. Ray S. Cline, *Secrets, Spies and Scholars: Blueprint of the Essential CIA* (Washington, D.C.: Acropolis, 1976), p. 226.

7. Prados, p. 403.

8. Interviewed in *U.S. News & World Report* and quoted by Allan E. Goodman in "Does Covert Action Have a Future?," *Parameters,* June 1988, p. 77.

9. *Amnesty International Report 1988* (London: Amnesty International, 1988), p. 114.

10. Speech to the Senate, March 4, 1988.

11. Victor Marchetti and John D. Marks, *The CIA and the Cult of Intelligence* (New York: Knopf, 1974), p. 377.

12. Gregory F. Treverton, *Covert Action: The Limits of Intervention in the Postwar World* (New York: Basic Books, 1987), p. 12.

13. Interviewed on *America's Century: Imperial Masquerade* (Channel 4 Television, 1989).

14. William R. Corson, *The Armies of Ignorance* (New York: Dial Press/James Wade, 1977), p. 521.

15. William Colby and Peter Forbath, *Honorable Men: My Life in the CIA* (New York: Simon and Schuster, 1978), p. 202.

16. Marchetti and Marks, p. 114.

17. Interviewed on *Secret Intelligence,* a three-part television documentary (copyright 1988 by Community Television of Southern California), which was shown over public television on various dates.

18. Ibid.

19. These words are from the Doolittle Report, as quoted on *Secret Intelligence.*

20. See *Alleged Assassination Plots Involving Foreign Leaders,* an interim report of the Church Committee, 94th Congress, 1st Session (Washington, D.C.: U.S. Government Printing Office, 1975).

21. *Secret Intelligence.*

22. Treverton, p. 24.

23. Ibid., p. 229.

24. Colby and Forbath, p. 410.

25. John Stockwell, *In Search of Enemies: A CIA Story* (New York: Norton, 1978), p. 10.

26. See Treverton, p. 116.

27. Bob Woodward, *Veil: The Secret Wars of the CIA, 1981–87* (New York: Pocket Books, 1987), pp. 452–455.

28. Interviewed on *Spying for Uncle Sam,* NBC-Television, 1978.

29. Interviewed on *Secret Intelligence.*

CHAPTER EIGHT

1. Victor Marchetti and John D. Marks, *The CIA and the Cult of Intelligence* (New York: Knopf, 1974), p. 373.

2. Harry Rositzke, *The CIA's Secret Operations: Espionage, Counterespionage and Covert Action* (New York: Reader's Digest Press, 1977), p. 239.

3. John Prados, *Presidents' Secret Wars: CIA and Pentagon Covert Operations Since World War II* (New York: William Morrow, 1986), pp. 144–147.

4. Bob Woodward, *Veil: The Secret Wars of the CIA, 1981–87* (New York: Pocket Books, 1987), p. 538.

5. Carl Bernstein and Bob Woodward, *All the President's Men* (New York: Simon and Schuster, 1974), p. 133.

6. William Colby and Peter Forbath, *Honorable Men: My Life in the CIA* (New York: Simon and Schuster, 1978), p. 327–328.

7. Thomas Powers, *The Man Who Kept the Secrets: Richard Helms and the CIA* (New York: Knopf, 1979), p. 260.

8. Ibid., p. 372.

9. Marchetti and Marks, p. 226.

10. Rositzke, p. 238.

11. For a detailed account of the unraveling of the Watergate scandal, see Bernstein and Woodward.

12. Prados, p. 336.

13. Interviewed on *Secret Intelligence*, a three-part television documentary (copyright 1988 by Community Television of Southern California) broadcast on public television on various dates.

14. The Hughes-Ryan Amendment and other key oversight legislation are summarized in Richard F. Grimmett, "Covert Actions: Congressional Oversight," a Congressional Research Service Issue Brief, CRS, Library of Congress, Washington, D.C., updated March 23, 1989.

15. Ellen Collier, "The War Powers Resolution: A Decade of Experience," Report 84–22F of the Congressional Research of the Library of Congress, p. 16.

16. Address to the Senate, March 4, 1988, reprinted in *Congressional Digest,* December 1988, p. 296.

17. See Seymour M. Hersh, "Who's in Charge Here?," *New York Times Magazine,* November 22, 1987, p. 35 and on.

18. Woodward, p. 247.

19. Ibid., p. 316.

20. Grimmett, p. 9.

21. William L. Chaze and others, "Inside the Shadow Network," *U.S. News & World Report,* December 15, 1986, p. 28.

22. Grimmett, p. 5.
23. Ibid., p. 13.
24. John Felton, "Wright Shelves Covert-Action Notice Bill," *Congressional Quarterly*, Weekly Report, February 4, 1989, p. 224.
25. Senator Patrick Leahy, speaking to the Senate on March 4, 1988, published in *Congressional Digest*, December 1988, p. 296.
26. Interviewed on National Public Radio, October 27, 1989.
27. Speech to the Senate, March 4, 1988, published in *Congressional Digest*, December 1988, p. 298.
28. Allan E. Goodman, "Does Covert Action Have a Future?," *Parameters*, June 1988, p. 80.
29. Speech to the Senate, March 4, 1988, published in *Congressional Digest*, December 1988, p. 298.

FOR FURTHER READING

In addition to the sources mentioned in the Source Notes, readers might be interested in exploring some of the following:

Bloch, Jonathan, and Patrick Fitzgerald. *British Intelligence and Covert Action.* Dublin, Ireland: Brandon Books, 1983.

Cave Brown, Anthony. *The Secret War Report of the OSS.* New York: Berkley Medallion, 1976).

da Silva, Peer. *Sub Rosa: The CIA and the Uses of Intelligence.* New York: Times Books, 1987.

Dziak, John J. *Chekisty: A History of the KGB.* New York: Ivy Books, 1988.

Elliot-Bateman, Michael, ed. *The Fourth Dimension of Warfare.* Vol. 1, *Intelligence/Subversion/Resistance.* Manchester, England: Manchester University Press, 1970.

Hunt, E. Howard. *Undercover.* Berkley-Putnam's, 1974.

Smith, Bradley F. *The Shadow Warriors: O.S.S. and the Origins of the C.I.A.* New York: Basic Books, 1983.

Turner, Stansfield. *Secrecy and Democracy: The CIA in Transition.* Boston: Houghton Mifflin, 1985.

White, Richard Alan. *The Morass: United States Intervention in Central America.* New York: Harper and Row, 1984.

INDEX